WORRY LESS PRAY MORE

WORRY LESS PRAY MORE

A Woman's
Devotional
Guide to
Anxiety-Free
Living

Donna K. Maltese

BARBOUR
PUBLISHING

ISBN 978-1-63609-422-9

Published by Barbour Publishing, Inc., 1810 Barbour Drive, Uhrichsville, Ohio 44683, www.barbourbooks.com

Our mission is to inspire the world with the life-changing message of the Bible.

Member of the
Evangelical Christian
Publishers Association

Printed in China.

INTRODUCTION

When we look at our troubles from our perspective, we're filled with dread and anxiety for they seem insurmountable. That's why—and when—we need to hand them over to God. We know He has all the power, strength, and wisdom to handle our worries for us. He'll find a solution we've never considered. He'll transform our situation into something good.

To remind us to worry less and pray more, the apostle Paul wrote:

> *Don't fret or worry. Instead of worrying, pray. Let petitions and praises shape your worries into prayers, letting God know your concerns. Before you know it, a sense of God's wholeness, everything coming together for good, will come and settle you down. It's wonderful what happens when Christ displaces worry at the center of your life.*
> PHILIPPIANS 4:6–7 MSG

Within this book, today's woman will find 180 readings and scripture passages to help her live a worry-free life while building up her prayer power as she learns to commit her concerns to the Master problem-solver.

Enter here to find your way to God's calming peace and bountiful provision.

TWENTY-FOUR-HOUR SECURITY

*Where can I find help? My help comes from the L*ORD*,*
*the maker of heaven and earth. . . . The L*ORD *guards*
*you from every evil. He guards your life. The L*ORD
guards you as you come and go, now and forever.
PSALM 121:1–2, 7–8 GW

Imagine having a bodyguard with you twenty-four hours a day. One who is all-powerful, all-knowing. He can see the future, the present, and the past. He never sleeps or takes catnaps. He blocks the sun from scorching your skin during the day and keeps the moon's shadows from tripping you up at night. He tightly grips your hand as you walk, shielding you from all harm.

You *have* such a bodyguard. His name is God. He's all the help and protection you need. So why worry? With the Creator of the universe guarding you, surrounding you with His magnificent presence and power, nothing can touch you—in heaven or on the earth!

· ·

I rest easy, Lord, knowing You are always with me, keeping
me from harm. Thank You for your vigilance and protection!

CULTIVATING CALM

*I've cultivated a quiet heart. Like a baby content in
its mother's arms, my soul is a baby content.*
PSALM 131:2 MSG

Psalm 131 was written by King David, who trained himself to trust
God, to put all things in His hands. David saw God as a stable,
ever-present, and powerful force for good and right in his life.

That's why David could say, "My soul waits calmly for God alone"
(Psalm 62:1 GW). He looked for no other outside influence—no
people, strong horses, tools, weapons, or money—to rescue
him. To firm that up within himself, he'd talk to his soul: "Wait
calmly for God alone, my soul, because my hope comes from
him. He alone is my rock and my savior—my stronghold. I cannot
be shaken" (Psalm 62:5–6 GW).

You too can cultivate a quiet heart and calm soul by making
God your sole rock and stronghold. Pray to Him and remind
yourself that He alone can—and will—handle everything that
comes your way.

. . . .

*You alone, Lord, are my Savior. Be calm,
my soul. Be content, my heart.*

GIVING—AND GETTING—PLEASURE

Be energetic in your life of salvation. . . . That energy is God's energy, an energy deep within you, God himself willing and working at what will give him the most pleasure.
PHILIPPIANS 2:12–13 MSG

Worrying can sap all your energy, using up all your strength and making you too bleary-eyed to see God's blessings, too weak to do what God's called you to do!

Dear woman, God didn't save you so that you could spend your life half asleep. He wants you to be strong, steady, and stable. So tell God all your concerns, all your imaginary what-ifs. Dig deep within, recognizing God's presence energizing you and giving you the power to let your worries melt away. Then open your eyes, and you'll see all the great tasks and blessings God has put before you.

The more you let go of your problems and pick up God's power, the more you'll please both God and yourself.

. . . .

I'm digging deep, Lord, freeing my frets and experiencing Your awesome energy! What pleasure!

PEACE FROM THE INSIDE OUT

"Your threat means nothing to us. If you throw us in the fire, the God we serve can rescue us. . . . But even if he doesn't, it wouldn't make a bit of difference, O king. We still wouldn't serve your gods or worship the gold statue you set up."
DANIEL 3:16–18 MSG

Shadrach, Meshach, and Abednego refused to worship King Nebuchadnezzar's idol, so he threatened to throw them into a furnace. But the three men refused to lose their peace. They knew God could rescue them. And if He didn't, so be it.

Warren Wiersbe wrote, "We're prone to want God to change our circumstances, but He wants to change our character. We think peace comes from the outside in, but it comes from the inside out."

No matter what your circumstances, don't let your fears and anxieties get the best of you. Keep your faith and your peace. You may have to walk through fire, but Christ will be there with you, and you'll come out unharmed (see Daniel 3:25–29)!

. . . .

Lord, here I am, claiming and holding on to Your eternal peace.

BLESSINGS TO GOD'S BELOVED

Except the Lord builds the house, they labor in vain
who build it. . . . It is vain for you to rise up early,
to take rest late, to eat the bread of [anxious] toil—
for He gives [blessings] to His beloved in sleep.
PSALM 127:1–2 AMPC

God wants His daughters to be useful. But without God's blessing on your work or ministry, not only will all your efforts be useless, but you will find yourself exhausted, eating the "bread of [anxious] toil," "work[ing] your worried fingers to the bone" (PSALM 127:2 MSG).

To live and work a worry-free life, ask God how He'd like you to use the gifts with which you've been blessed. Then follow where He leads, taking on the job or ministry He's directing you toward.

Once you're in the space God has provided, invite Him into every moment of your workday. Put your efforts and their outcome in His hands. Then you'll have the peace and rest God is so willing and able to give those He loves.

· ·

I'm resting in You, Lord, my provider, my love.

10

NOTHING TOO HARD FOR GOD

Alas, Lord God! Behold, You have made the heavens and the earth by Your great power and by Your outstretched arm! There is nothing too hard or too wonderful for You.
JEREMIAH 32:17 AMPC

Sometimes the many things going *right* in your life and your world are overshadowed by that one thing that's going wrong. You begin to question whether God has the power or know-how to change things for the better or get you out of whatever mess you're in.

That's when you need to begin focusing on the right things. Trust that along with all the wonderful things God has done, is doing, and will do, He will turn any mishaps, errors, or darkness into something right, correct, and light.

You see, there is nothing too hard for God. He can do anything, so don't panic. Simply pray, and leave everything in God's mighty hands.

. . . .

Thank You, God, for reminding me nothing is too hard for You. I'm leaving everything up to You, knowing You'll put things right.

NEVER SHAKEN

*Those who trust the L*ORD *are like Mount Zion,*
which can never be shaken. It remains firm forever.
As the mountains surround Jerusalem, so the
L*ORD surrounds his people now and forever.*
PSALM 125:1–2 GW

Sometimes worry can lead you to literally shake in your boots, but God wants you to know that if you trust in Him, you will *never* be shaken. You can stand firm, leaning on His power, confidently hoping He has a solution, one you've never even thought of—or, even better, that He's already taking care of things for you!

When you put all your trust, hope, and confidence in the God who actually *created* the mountains, you begin to feel His awesome presence surrounding you. You begin remembering all the things He has done for you and all the others who've gone before you. Knowing this, you need no longer shake in your boots but walk sure and barefooted on the highest mountains (see Psalm 18:33).

. . . .

I'm trusting in You, Lord. In doing so, I feel Your power and presence surrounding me, enabling me to walk strong in You.

A MATTER OF COURSE

*"So don't worry and don't keep saying, 'What shall we
eat, what shall we drink or what shall we wear?!' . . .
[Y]our Heavenly Father knows that you need them all.
Set your heart on the kingdom and his goodness, and all
these things will come to you as a matter of course."*
MATTHEW 6:31–33 PHILLIPS

The apostle Paul, the author of Philippians, wasn't the first one
to come up with the idea of praying instead of worrying (see
Philippians 4:6–7). It was Jesus!

First, Jesus taught His followers how to pray. Then He said,
"Stop being perpetually uneasy (anxious and worried) about your
life" (Matthew 6:25 AMPC). Do not be worried about what you'll
eat, drink, or wear, for doing so will not make things any better.
Besides, your God *knows* what you need.

Your duty is to seek God more than anything—or anyone—else,
knowing and trusting that if you will but ask, you *will* receive!

. . . .

*Help me, Lord, to find a way to put my concerns in Your
hands, knowing You'll find a way when I see no way!*

A STUDENT OF PRAYER

*Then He was praying in a certain place; and when He
stopped, one of His disciples said to Him, Lord, teach us
to pray. . . . And He said to them, When you pray, say:
Our Father Who is in heaven, hallowed be Your name.*
LUKE 11:1–2 AMPC

The disciples had witnessed the power, joy, and wisdom Jesus
exuded in their presence. They'd also seen Him go off alone to
pray. So one asked Him, "Lord, teach us to pray."

Through the example of Jesus and His disciples, it's clear that
prayer is the antidote to worry. For the stronger you are in prayer,
the less your concerns will weigh you down.

Today, come to Jesus as a willing and worthy student. Ask
Him to teach you how to weaken your worries and build up your
faith as you learn to pray with power. Start with the basics. Pray
this "Disciples' Prayer" (see Luke 11:2–4), knowing Abba God is
longing to hear what you have to say.

. . . .

*Abba God, hear my prayer.
"Our Father Who is in heaven. . ."*

THAT SECRET PLACE

When you pray, go into your [most] private room, and, closing the door, pray to your Father, Who is in secret; and your Father, Who sees in secret, will reward you in the open.
MATTHEW 6:6 AMPC

Women living in today's world are busy, and chances are, you're no exception. There are kids to get on the bus, socks to find for the husband, emails to send, projects to finish, meals to plan, grandkids to watch, Sunday school lessons to review, dogs to walk, and news to catch up on. Yet to be focused enough to do all these things well, you need to unload some of the clutter crowding your mind.

Jesus tells you to detach from the world without and the thoughts within—to find that secret chamber He's opened just for you where you can have a spirit-to-Spirit talk with God, shutting yourself away from the world and shutting yourself in with Him.

Find that place and you'll find your reward—the focus to do and the peace to be!

. . . .

*Father, help me find that secret place
where it's just You and me.*

GIVING GOD THE DETAILS

*Hezekiah took the letters from the messengers, read them, and went to the L*ORD*'s temple. He spread them out in front of the L*ORD *and prayed to the L*ORD*.*
2 KINGS 19:14–15 GW

Hezekiah was the king of Judah. Here we find he's received letters filled with threats of attack from Sennacherib of Assyria. After reading the letters, Hezekiah didn't panic but went to the temple of the Lord. There he spread out the threatening messages before the Lord and prayed, acknowledging God as the supreme Ruler and Creator of heaven and earth. He asked God to listen to him, to open His ears and hear Sennacherib's message, and to come to the rescue of His people. And God did.

When you have a massive problem, don't panic. Go to God, and then lay all the details before Him. Ask Him to save you. And He will.

. . . .

Lord of all, here's what's happening. . . I'm resolved not to panic but to come to You, for in You alone will I find help.

WORTHY THOUGHTS

Keep your thoughts on whatever is right or deserves praise: things that are true, honorable, fair, pure, acceptable, or commendable.
PHILIPPIANS 4:8 GW

It's easy to get caught up in the bad news that surrounds us: the reports and rumors of wars, school shootings, child and spousal abuse, drug addiction, crime, terrorism, and political strife, to name just a few. It's enough to make you never come out from underneath the covers. Either that or you find yourself forever fretting about people and situations over which you have no or little control. Yet you can't help but be concerned.

So take those news items to God. Ask Him to be in the situation, to help the victims, to bring justice. Then leave it all in His hands, knowing He can handle anything—and everything. Then look for some *good* news stories—they are out there! And fix your focus on *those* things, which are good, honorable, and commendable, praising God in the process.

. . . .

Once I give my concerns to You, Lord, help me fix my thoughts on those things that deserve my praise and focus! Amen.

REASSURANCE TIMES THREE

You know when I leave and when I get back; I'm never out of your sight. . . . I look behind me and you're there, then up ahead and you're there, too—your reassuring presence, coming and going. This is too much, too wonderful.
PSALM 139:2, 5–6 MSG

People come and go out of your life, but there is a three-in-one person who remains: God, Jesus, and the Holy Spirit.

Wherever you go, God sees you. Whatever you're experiencing, Jesus is familiar with it. Whatever comfort you need, the Spirit is there, giving it to you. When you believe these things, when you have faith in God's presence always with you—before and behind you—all worries fade away. God is your reassuring Protector, Jesus your undying Friend, and the Spirit your willing Helper.

Don't worry. Pray to these three supernatural powers who are ready, willing, and able to help you along the way.

. . . .

My worries fade, Lord, and vanish into nothing when I acknowledge Your presence, Jesus' love, and the Spirit's power. Be with me now.

THE ONE WHO COMFORTS

"I, yes I, am the one who comforts you.
So why are you afraid of mere humans,
who wither like the grass and disappear?"
Isaiah 51:12 NLT

God understands you like no other. He knows your worries, fears, hopes, dreams, and passions. He sees what's going on in your life. That's why Father God wants to fill you, His daughter, with assurance that He alone is the One who can and does comfort you. He is all-powerful and eternal, unlike humans, who'll one day fade away, wither like the grass, and become as nothing.

So when you are worried or fearful about what some person might say or do next, draw close to the "one who comforts you" like no other. Lean into God, His power, promises, and protection. Remind yourself of who He is and the solace He and His presence provide. Allow His love and light to pour over you as you pray.

. . . .

Abba God, pour Your love, light, and protection over me.
In You I find the comfort that melts all fears and worries.

TRUSTING THE MASTER PLANNER

Blessed is the person who places his confidence in the LORD and does not rely on arrogant people or those who follow lies. You have done many miraculous things, O LORD my God. You have made many wonderful plans for us. No one compares to you!
PSALM 40:4–5 GW

You've made a few plans, but it feels like it's taking forever for things to fall into place. You begin listening to others, finding yourself tempted to follow their advice. Before you know it, you're worrying, wringing your hands, wondering if you should take another track or give up your plans altogether.

If you're not sure you're on the right path, share your concerns with the Master Planner. Place all your trust in Him, relying on His wisdom, for He's already done some marvelous things in your life. If your plans are aligned with His will and Word, you can rest easy. He'll give you the patience and peace you need to see things through—in His time and way.

. . . .

*You have many wonderful plans for me, Lord.
I'm trusting You'll help me see them through.*

INSIDE THE CIRCLE OF PROTECTION

GOD met me more than halfway, he freed me from my anxious fears. . . . When I was desperate, I called out, and GOD got me out of a tight spot. GOD's angel sets up a circle of protection around us while we pray.
PSALM 34:4, 6–7 MSG

When you're weighed down by anxiety, God is ready to meet you "more than halfway." All you need to do is cry out to Him; tell Him everything that's on your mind, all your fears, worries, and troubles. "Never hide your feelings from him" (Psalm 34:5 MSG). Although God knows what you're fearing and worrying about and all the troubles in your midst, He wants you to voice them, to unload them upon Him, to get them out of your system.

Once you do, God will rescue you and fill you with His peace; His angel will set up a protective circle around you until you are able to rise up again in strength. Don't neglect the privilege and benefit of prayer. It's a life saver.

. . . .

Here's what's happening, Lord. . . Save me!

THE FATHER WHO LISTENS

I love the LORD because he hears my voice and my prayer for mercy. Because he bends down to listen, I will pray as long as I have breath!
PSALM 116:1–2 NLT

Listening has almost become a lost art among humans. But there's one person who will *always* pay attention to what you have to say: God—a supernatural, all-powerful Father who actually *bends down to listen* to what you, His daughter, is saying!

Fix firmly in your mind that image of God bending down to you. See yourself as the woman-child that so desperately needs her Father to hear all her woes and worries. Why like a child? Because "the LORD protects those of childlike faith" (Psalm 116:6 NLT).

When you put all your trust in Father God, when you tell Him that you believe in Him and are deeply troubled (see Psalm 116:10), you'll come away free from fretting, and your soul will "be at rest again" (Psalm 116:7 NLT).

. . . .

Lord, I want the soul-rest only You can supply. Listen. . .

THE BIG ASK

"Ask and it will be given to you. Search and you will find. Knock and the door will be opened for you. The one who asks will always receive; the one who is searching will always find, and the door is opened to the man who knocks."
MATTHEW 7:7–8 PHILLIPS

In these days of information overload, your mind is likely overcluttered with various what-if scenarios swirling around in your head. It's likely that you're not even conscious of all these unchecked worries.

Fortunately, you have a Father God who can give you peace of mind, heart, spirit, and soul. As His daughter, you have the privilege to come before Him in prayer.

Jesus says that when you give God your worries and **A**sk for His peace, you'll get it. If you **S**eek the Father's presence, you'll find Him. If you **K**nock on the door of His home and love, He'll open it to you.

Ask, Seek, and Knock (ASK)—and be blessed with clarity, peace, and hope.

. . . .

Here I am, Lord, giving, asking, seeking, and knocking. Hear my prayer.

OUT OF SELF AND INTO JESUS

Jesus. . .said to them, If anyone intends to come after Me, let him deny himself [forget, ignore, disown, and lose sight of himself and his own interests] and take up his cross, and . . .follow with Me [continually, cleaving steadfastly to Me].

MARK 8:34 AMPC

Some worries are egocentric. You worry you won't be promoted, you won't get the house you bid on, you'll never get ahead monetarily, and so on. In this land of worry, it's all about you. But Jesus wants you to realize it's really all about Him and that if you want to be His follower, you're to lose sight of yourself and your own interests.

That's a tall order, but it is possible and so much more freeing than fretting. When you empty yourself of your concerns, you have more room to hold what God wants to give you.

Get out of yourself and into Jesus. You'll find you won't regret it.

. . . .

Jesus, help me focus on You alone. I want to get out of myself and into You!

PROOF OF THE PROMISE

And how bold and free we then become in his presence, freely asking according to his will, sure that he's listening. And if we're confident that he's listening, we know that what we've asked for is as good as ours.
1 JOHN 5:14–15 MSG

In Mark 11:24, Jesus said that you'll get what you ask for if you really believe. Such a promise was proven by an account of a woman who'd been bleeding for twelve years. She'd been to lots of doctors and still was not whole. Hearing Jesus was coming, she sneaked up to Him, saying to herself, "If I only touch his garment, I will be made well" (Matthew 9:21 ESV). Jesus saw her and said, "Take heart, daughter; your faith has made you well" (Matthew 9:22 ESV). And in that instant, she was!

Take your concerns to God. Let Him know your desires. Then leave all in His hands, believing that He's listened and what you've asked for is already yours—and it will be.

. . . .

Jesus, You prove the promises, so I'm bringing You all my concerns, knowing what You will for me is already mine.

EXPECT THE UNEXPECTED

*Seeing Peter and John about to go into the temple, he asked
to receive alms. And Peter directed his gaze at him, as
did John, and said, "Look at us." And he fixed his attention
on them, expecting to receive something from them.*
ACTS 3:3–5 ESV

When you bring your worries to God, chances are you also let Him
know how you'd like things worked out before you leave them all
in His hands. In other words, you let God know what you expect
to happen. But sometimes what you expect is not the best thing
for you.

Take the lame man sitting outside the temple. He expected
Peter and John to give him money. But they gave him something
else—healing in Jesus' name!

Rest assured that when you hand your troubles over to God,
He'll go deeper, to the very core of your desire, and discover
what you really want. Expect God to give you the unexpected,
the better thing.

. . . .

*Lord, when I give You my concerns,
help me expect the unexpected!*

BECOMING A BLESSING

The LORD said to Abram, "Leave your land, your relatives, and your father's home. Go to the land that I will show you. I will make you a great nation, I will bless you. I will make your name great, and you will be a blessing."
GENESIS 12:1–2 GW

Chances are that most of your worries are about you and your own life, and that's only normal. But after you've come to God in prayer and dropped your worries off with Him, He would have you leave the land of You-ville behind and come into the land He'll show you—the one where it's all about God and others.

Freed up from your own concerns, you now have room and time to bring to God the concerns of others. That's you following Jesus and using the kingdom power of prayer on behalf of others. That's you becoming a blessing to others and God, continuing the work your Master started.

God's ready to go. Are you?

. . . .

I have friends I'd like to bring to You today, Abba. They need Your blessing.

POWER AND PEACE ARE YOURS

The LORD will give power to his people.
The LORD will bless his people with peace.
PSALM 29:11 GW

The statements above are so simple. Yet they're filled with power.

God is Ruler over all. And you're His daughter, one of "his people." Thus, on days when you're weakened by worry, you can go to God for all the strength you need. He'll give you the power to persevere and prevail. And, good daughter, He'll also bless you with peace in this very moment and all the moments to come.

There's only one caveat. You need to *believe*, to fix these facts firmly in your mind so you'll not feel helpless and veer from the path He's laid out for you.

So drop your worries by the doorstep as you enter God's presence. Take in all the strength and peace, which He's *always* waiting to give you. And go on your way in His name and power.

. . . .

Lord, my God and King, I come into Your presence. Fill me with Your power and peace so I may do Your will.

GETTING IN HARMONY WITH GOD

*"Be in harmony and at peace with God. In this way
you will have prosperity. Accept instruction from
his mouth, and keep his words in your heart."*
JOB 22:21–22 GW

When you're caught up in a cycle of worry and anxiety, you're not in harmony with God. On top of that, your fretting begins to become a barrier between you and Him. This keeps you from receiving the full power, strength, and peace God aches to give you.

Today, get back in harmony with God. Put your trust in the words and promises of the love letter (the Bible) He's written just for you. Ingest His wisdom and follow it, allowing it to have full sway over your thoughts. Don't just *write* His words on your heart; *keep* them there so when worry flares up, you can quench it with God's wisdom. In so doing, you'll find yourself prospering more than you ever dreamed or imagined.

. . . .

*I want Your song in my heart, Lord. Help me leave my
worry behind as I get myself back in harmony with You.*

GETTING A FAITH-LIFT

Anxiety in a man's heart weighs him down,
but a good word makes him glad.
PROVERBS 12:25 ESV

Worry is a weight that presses upon your heart. That's why the psalmist wrote that you should "Pile your troubles on GOD's shoulders—he'll carry your load, he'll help you out" (Psalm 55:22 MSG). That's why Jesus told you not to be anxious about anything but come to Him if you're heavy laden; that He'll give you the rest you need (see Matthew 6:25; 11:28–29). That's why Peter reminds you to "Give all your worries and cares to God, for he cares about you" (1 Peter 5:7 NLT).

But where's a modern woman to obtain that "good word" she needs to make her glad? In God's Word. Find a verse, psalm, or story that speaks to your heart—and make it part of *your* story. When you do, you'll find yourself lifted up to the heavenly God who waits to greet you.

. . . .

My heart is heavy, Lord, so I'm digging into Your Word.
Reveal the words I need to lift me up to You!

CONFIDENCE IN GOD

*I know and rest in confidence upon it that the
Lord will maintain the cause of the afflicted,
and will secure justice for the poor and needy.*
PSALM 140:12 AMPC

According to headlines, evil and violence appear to be on the rise. Hearing all the bad news that's out there, you may find yourself worrying not only about your own safety but about the safety of others, as well as justice for the afflicted. It's almost too much to take in! Yet you weren't meant or designed to do so.

Your only recourse is to just hand those suffering over to God and to rest in the confidence that *He* will take care of all those harmed by evil and violence. That *He* will see justice for His children. It may not happen tomorrow, in your lifetime, or on this side of heaven, but it will happen. In God's time and way.

Meanwhile, begin lifting up to God all those who are troubled, and leave the outcome in His hands.

. . . .

*Lord, I'm handing over the afflicted to You.
Heal their hearts, and bring them justice.*

GOD IS NEAR

The LORD is close to the brokenhearted;
he rescues those whose spirits are crushed.
PSALM 34:18 NLT

Human beings are fragile creatures. As one such being, your heart can break, your spirit be crushed. It can happen after hearing mean words from someone or suffering the betrayal of someone you counted on and trusted. Maybe it happened upon the death of a loved one. Perhaps it was the loss of a job, a house, a business, a pastor, a friend. Whatever the cause, upon the heels of a broken heart and a crushed spirit, anxiety is sure to follow. You wonder, *Why did it happen? How do I go on from here?*

Know that in the midst of trial, God is right there with you. He's holding you in His arms. He'll heal your heart, restore your spirit, and alleviate your anxiety. You need say nothing more than, "Lord. . .help me."

. . . .

Thank You, Lord, for always being there when I need
You. You're the one sure thing I can count on. You will
heal my heart, revive my spirit, and calm my soul.

BELIEVE AND LOOK

[What, what would have become of me] had I not believed that I would see the Lord's goodness in the land of the living! Wait and hope for and expect the Lord; be brave and of good courage. . . . Yes, wait for and hope for and expect the Lord.
PSALM 27:13–14 AMPC

The AMPC translation above asks what would become of you if you didn't believe you'd see God's goodness in the world in which you're now living? If you let your worries and anxieties have complete sway over you, annihilating any hope that God *will do something* and *you will see* the results?

God's Word gives you a simple verse to memorize, to fortify your faith, and to give you hope when all seems hopeless: "I believe that I shall look upon the goodness of the LORD in the land of the living!" (Psalm 27:13 ESV). That's a simple verse to memorize, fortifying your faith and giving you hope when all seems hopeless. Make it part of your arsenal. Determine to look to God with complete dependence and trust. Then you'll find the strength and courage to get through anything.

. . . .

I expect to see Your goodness, Lord, in this land. This gives me hope!

YOUR HIDING PLACE

For you are my hiding place; you protect me from trouble. You surround me with songs of victory.
PSALM 32:7 NLT

Physically, it's difficult to find a place where you can truly hide. Someone will always find you, whether it be the kids, the boss, the husband, or the boyfriend. It's almost as if their radar goes off whenever you want to find a moment alone.

Yet spiritually there is one place you can always go to get away from all people and all worry. It's in God's presence. Once you're there, you find yourself surrounded with not just love and encouragement but with songs of victory.

God is your biggest cheerleader and best coach. He says, "I will guide you along the best pathway for your life. I will advise you and watch over you" (Psalm 32:8 NLT). His only caveat is for you not to be stubborn when He tells you which way to go, what to do. But that's a small price to pay to live in victory.

. . . .

Lord, I come to hide in You. Save me, guide me. Make me putty in Your hands.

GOD'S COMMAND FOR YOU

*"This is my command—be strong and courageous!
Do not be afraid or discouraged. For the LORD
your God is with you wherever you go."*
JOSHUA 1:9 NLT

Moses has died, and Joshua is left to lead God's people into the Promised Land. Can you imagine all the thoughts that must have been going through Joshua's head? Perhaps that's why God tells him three times to be strong and courageous and two times that He would be with him (see Joshua 1:5–9).

Chances are your challenges are not as great as Joshua's. But even if they are, these are the words God wants you to take to heart. Forget about worrying. That will only sap your energy and courage. Instead, know with certainty that God *is* with you. He will *never* leave you. No matter where you go, God is there. So be strong and brave. God's got you.

. . . .

*Thank You, Lord, for these encouraging words. Help me
get them through my head so that I can be the strong
and courageous woman You've designed me to be!*

KEEP GOING

I do not consider myself to have "arrived",
spiritually, nor do I consider myself already perfect.
But I keep going on, grasping ever more firmly
that purpose for which Christ grasped me.
PHILIPPIANS 3:13 PHILLIPS

Do you sometimes worry about the things you've said and done? It's time to leave the past in the past. God knows you aren't perfect. That's why He sent Jesus and then left you His Spirit, so that you'd have supernatural help on your journey through life.

So don't let would'ves, could'ves, and should'ves rule your life. Just keep going, leaving the outcome of all things to God. Don't look behind, worrying about the ramifications of your words and actions. Hand them over to God. Then "leave the past behind and with hands outstretched to whatever lies ahead. . .go straight for the goal," heading for the "reward. . .of being called by God in Christ" (Philippians 3:14 PHILLIPS).

· ·

Jesus, please help me leave the past in the past.
I don't want to be like Lot's wife (see Luke 17:32),
frozen where I stand. Help me move forward toward You.

THORNS OF WORRY AND RICHES

"The seed planted among thornbushes is another person who hears the word. But the worries of life and the deceitful pleasures of riches choke the word so that it can't produce anything."
MATTHEW 13:22 GW

Jesus tells a parable about a farmer who sows seed. The seed that fell on the path is grabbed up by birds (the evil one). The seed sown on the rocky ground quickly withered when the sun scorched it. These are people of little faith who lost their way when troubles came. The seeds that fell amid thorns got choked out. These are people who allowed the cares of the world and money to choke God's Word out of their life, making them unfruitful.

Your goal is to give your worries to God—not to focus on the treasures of this world, but to grow on God's Word, allowing it to build you up. Then you'll be the fruitful seed, yielding more crops than you ever thought possible.

God's waiting. Bloom where He's planted you.

· ·

Help me bear fruit for You, Lord, as I let go of my worries and take up Your Word.

POWER TOOLS

For God did not give us a spirit of timidity (of cowardice, of craven and cringing and fawning fear), but [He has given us a spirit] of power and of love and of calm and well-balanced mind and discipline and self-control.
2 TIMOTHY 1:7 AMPC

God doesn't want your worries to keep you cowering in the wings, afraid to step out on the stage, so He's gifted you with tools to help you live out a heavenly life while you're here on earth. He's given you a spirit of power, the same power He used to raise Jesus from the dead (see Philippians 3:10). He's filled you with the spirit of love, which prompts you to please God and put the welfare of others above your own. And He's given you a calm, well-balanced mind.

Use the power tools God has given you. Put worries behind as you pour yourself into God and construct a heaven on earth through prayer.

. . . .

Lord, thank You for the power tools of love and a calm mind. Help me use them to build up Your kingdom.

GOD'S PATHWAY FOR YOU

*Your road led through the sea, your pathway through
the mighty waters—a pathway no one knew was there!
You led your people along that road like a flock of
sheep, with Moses and Aaron as their shepherds.*
PSALM 77:19–20 NLT

Worries may come upon you like mighty waters. Once you were standing in the shallows, then you wandered deeper into the depths, and before you knew it, you were caught in the undertow. How would you ever regain your footing?

Before you let your worries pull you under, go to God. Ask Him to show you the pathway you cannot see with your limited vision. He will clearly reveal the road He's carved out just for you, the path He's provided by dividing waters, obliterating the worry and despair that blocks your way. Then He'll calm you, take you by the hand, and carefully and masterfully guide you as any good and loving shepherd would.

. . . .

*I don't want these worries to take me under,
Lord. Calm my soul. Take my hand. Lead me,
Good Shepherd, to safety and hope.*

EQUIPPED BY GOD

Then David took his shepherd's staff, selected five smooth stones from the brook, and put them in the pocket of his shepherd's pack, and with his sling in his hand approached Goliath.

1 SAMUEL 17:40 MSG

Do you sometimes worry you're not equipped to face the challenges before you?

David didn't. He was just a young shepherd boy when he convinced King Saul that God would help him defeat Goliath. And when Saul tried to outfit David in kingly armor, David said, "I can't even move with all this stuff on me. I'm not used to this" (1 Samuel 17:39 MSG). So he took it off and donned his usual gear: his trust in God, a staff, stones, and a sling. With these, David took down the giant.

Just as God equipped David to defeat Goliath, God's given you exactly what you need to face your own challenges. So leave your worries in His hands, take up the weapon of prayer, don your usual gear, and you too will win the battle.

. . . .

Thank You, Lord, for giving me all I need to face the challenges before me.

AT HOME IN GOD

You've taken my hand. You wisely and tenderly lead me,
and then you bless me. . . . I'm in the very presence of GOD—
oh, how refreshing it is! I've made Lord GOD my home.
PSALM 73:23–24, 28 MSG

When you worry you'll never find your way, take a look at where you're standing. Have you moved away from God?

Remember the Lord is your rock, fortress, and shelter. When you get close to Him in prayer, He'll take your hand and lead you exactly where you need to go, and then He'll bless you as soon as your feet touch down on the path He's opened up for you.

Today, get yourself into the presence of God. Allow Him to take your hand. As you do, you'll not only find the refreshment you've been thirsting for but the home your spirit and soul have been longing for—in Him alone.

. . . .

Lord, when doubts and worries assail me, help me get back
to You, my only true home in this world and the next.

GOD CALLS YOU AS HE SEES YOU

The angel of the LORD appeared to him and
said, "Mighty hero, the LORD is with you!"
JUDGES 6:12 NLT

The Midianites kept taking all the crops God's people had sown. So Gideon was threshing wheat in a winepress, hiding his grain from the Midianite raiders. That's when God came and called him a "mighty hero."

Yet Gideon denied God's estimation of him, telling God he was the least in his family and his clan the weakest of its tribe. But God told Gideon He was sending him, that Gideon was to go in the strength he had. God would be with him, and he would defeat the enemy. (See Judges 6:14–16.)

When you worry you aren't good enough to do what God has called you to do, go to Him in prayer. He'll remind you who you are, a mighty hero, a daughter of God. Your job is to believe Him, to trust Him to empower you. Then you'll become the woman God sees you already are.

. . . .

Help me see myself through Your eyes,
Lord, a mighty daughter of a mighty God.

GOD HAS A FIRM GRIP ON YOU

"Don't panic. I'm with you. There's no need to fear for I'm your God. I'll give you strength. I'll help you. I'll hold you steady, keep a firm grip on you. Count on it: Everyone who had it in for you will end up out in the cold—real losers."
Isaiah 41:10–11 MSG

Isaiah 41:10–13 are wonderful verses to take hold of when worry turns to fear and then panic. They are words spoken by your God, who knows all things that have happened, are happening, and will happen to you.

God tells you not to panic because He is with you. He'll give you all the strength you need to face whatever lies before you. He has your hand, and He'll never let you go. He'll keep you steady on your feet, give you firm footing to walk where He'd have you go. And those who threaten you today will be gone tomorrow.

Believe, and you will have the strength and peace your heart, spirit, and soul crave.

. . . .

Lord, in You I find my courage. I'm counting on You alone!

PONDERING GOD

*I meditate on all Your doings; I ponder the work
of Your hands. . . . Cause me to hear Your loving-
kindness in the morning, for on You do I lean and in
You do I trust. Cause me to know the way wherein
I should walk, for I lift up my inner self to You.*
PSALM 143:5, 8 AMPC

One surefire way to keep worry at bay is to go to God in the morning, before your feet hit the floor, before your mind has a chance to wander into dangerous doubts, fears, and imaginings.

Open God's Word or focus on tried-and-true verses that lift your thoughts and shield your mind. Remember all the great things God has done in the past, and thank Him for what He's doing in the present. Then lean in close. Tell God you trust Him. Ask Him to show you the way you're to go. Listen to what He says as you lift up your inner woman to Him, spirit to Spirit, love to Love.

. . . .

*I'm coming to You before all other things,
Lord. Love me, lead me, lift me to You.*

GOD TO THE RESCUE

*Though I am surrounded by troubles, you will protect
me from the anger of my enemies. You reach out
your hand, and the power of your right hand saves
me. The LORD will work out his plans for my life—
for your faithful love, O LORD, endures forever.*
PSALM 138:7–8 NLT

Sometimes life can surprise you. You're going along your merry
way, and then all of a sudden, before you know it, you're surrounded
by trouble. You're in the thick of a situation you never saw coming.
Now you're more than worried—you're ready to freak out!

Stop. Take a deep breath no matter where you are or what
you're doing. Remind yourself that God will—*is*—protecting
you. His power is saving you in that very moment. He's going to
work everything out for you. Why? Because He not only loves
you but has a good plan for your life. All you need to do is trust
Him and live it!

. . . .

*Protect me, Lord, when danger steals in.
I know You'll save me. You have a plan!*

PERFECT, TRUSTING PEACE

*You will keep in perfect peace all who trust in
you, all whose thoughts are fixed on you!*
Isaiah 26:3 nlt

Poet Kathleen Norris wrote, "Prayer is not asking for what you think you want, but asking to be changed in ways you can't imagine."

Wouldn't you love to be able to be calm, unflustered, serene no matter what comes your way? Can you even imagine what that would look like?

It is possible to have perfect peace. It's a simple formula to remember: The first part is to trust in God. That means committing yourself to Him and His ways, leaning on Him, hoping and expecting Him to move in your life. The second part is keeping your mind on Him. That means planting His Word deep within yourself, spending time with Him, and learning about who He is.

Ask God to change you from a worrier to a woman of peace. He'll then do the unimaginable—to your good and His glory!

. . . .

*Lord, I want the calm only You can provide. Change me,
Lord. Make me a woman of perfect, trusting peace.*

CONFESS AND REFRESH

So repent (change your mind and purpose); turn around and return [to God], that your sins may be erased (blotted out, wiped clean), that times of refreshing (of recovering from the effects of heat, of reviving with fresh air) may come from the presence of the Lord.
Acts 3:19 AMPC

If handing your worries over to God in prayer isn't bringing you peace, it may be you haven't told Him all that's been going on in your life. You haven't confessed those things you don't even want to admit to yourself. And so, they remain hidden within you, festering like an unclean wound.

Dear woman, nothing is hidden from God. He sees all you do, hears all you say (see Job 34:21). But if you want to be refreshed, to have less worry and more peace, ask God to examine you (Psalm 139:23–24). To reveal the hidden missteps you have yet to confess. Know that God *will* forgive you. And afterward you'll come away more refreshed than ever!

. . . .

Lord, look within me. Reveal the misstep that's keeping me anxious. Help me tell You all.

EXPERIENCING GOD'S
MANY ASPECTS

*Blessed be the Lord, my Rock and my keen
and firm Strength. . .my Steadfast Love and my
Fortress, my High Tower and my Deliverer,
my Shield and He in Whom I trust and take refuge.*
PSALM 144:1–2 AMPC

Your vision for your life, your day, seems a bit cloudy. You've prayed and you've prayed, and still you come away with some dregs of anxiety you can't seem to clear out. Perhaps it's time to go slow. To go deep. To experience who God truly is. To soothe your soul by acknowledging His many facets.

See God as your solid rock that will not be moved. Allow Him to be your strength. Recognize He is your steadfast love, forever and constant. He is your great protector, your fortress. In times of trouble, you can run to Him, your high tower, and be safe. He, your deliverer and ever-present shield, will rescue and protect you.

Trust and take refuge in God, your all in all.

· ·

*Today in You I'm going deep, Lord—my rock, strength,
steadfast love, fortress, high tower, deliverer, and shield.*

HABITUAL PRAYER

*Be earnest and unwearied and steadfast in
your prayer [life], being [both] alert and intent
in [your praying] with thanksgiving.*
COLOSSIANS 4:2 AMPC

If your prayer life is sporadic, your peace will be also. And if you don't pepper your petitions with thanksgiving, your prayers will become a mere litany of selfish desires you'd like fulfilled before you go on your way and in your own power.

That's why the apostle Paul, the author of Colossians, encourages you to pray continually from the heart and to make prayer a tireless habit in your life.

So don't go to God just once a day but throughout your day. When you see someone suffering, pray. When worry begins to creep into your mind, pray. While you're with God in all ways all day, thank Him for all He has done, is doing, and will do. In so doing, not only will all your worries fade, but you'll find yourself walking God's way and in His power.

. . . .

*Help me, Lord, to be steadfast in my prayer life,
continually giving thanks to You in all ways all day.*

GOD—THE CYCLE BREAKER

When I am afraid, I will put my trust in you. I praise God for what he has promised. . . . For you have rescued me from death; you have kept my feet from slipping. So now I can walk in your presence, O God, in your life-giving light.
PSALM 56:3–4, 13 NLT

Fear can cause anxiety, and anxiety can cause fear. It's a vicious cycle, but it's one God can break.

To steer clear of fear and to keep worry from taking over your life—the life God wants you to live in Him—you need to trust the One who rules and sustains the universe. That person is God.

When you're afraid, trust God. Remember all the promises He's made to you, including the fact that He goes before you and behind you. That He'll never, ever leave nor forsake you.

God has already sent Jesus to rescue you from death and given you the Holy Spirit to guide your feet. So trust Him. As you do, you'll be walking in His life-giving light!

. . . .

When I'm afraid, I'll trust in You, Lord!

A STACK OF BLESSINGS
WAITING FOR YOU

Desperate, I throw myself on you: you are my God! Hour by hour I place my days in your hand. . . . What a stack of blessing you have piled up for those who worship you, ready and waiting for all who run to you to escape an unkind world.
PSALM 31:14–15, 19 MSG

One good way to throw off worry is to throw yourself on God in the midst of it. Second by second, minute by minute, hour by hour, put yourself into the hands of the One who loves and protects you. The One who longs to talk to you, walk with you, and carry you when necessary.

No matter what your troubles or worries, God will find a unique way of making good come out of anything and everything that comes your way. So escape into God, knowing He has a stack of blessings waiting just for you.

· ·

My worries evaporate when I put myself in Your hands, Lord. In You a stack of blessings are waiting—just for me!

GOD'S RAINBOW IN THE CLOUDS

*"Whenever I form clouds over the earth, a rainbow
will appear in the clouds. Then I will remember
my promise to you and every living animal."*
GENESIS 9:14–15 GW

God was disappointed with the humans He'd created, so He sent floodwaters to destroy all living creatures—all except for Noah's family and the animals in the ark, of course. Afterward, regretting what He'd done, God told Noah the rainbow would be a sign of His promise to never again allow water to destroy all life.

God promises that He'll never give up on you no matter what you've done. He will be there for you no matter how great your flood of worries and troubles. Let God's beautiful rainbow amid the clouds be a reminder that He *will* make something good come out of the storms in your life (see Romans 8:28). Just look up to Him and His spectral arc. He's set something good for you amid your clouds.

. . . .

*Father God, thank You for making all things work for
good. Help me focus on Your rainbow amid my clouds.*

GOD'S GATEWAY OF HOPE

"I will lead her into the desert and speak tenderly to her there. I will return her vineyards to her and transform the Valley of Trouble into a gateway of hope."
HOSEA 2:14–15 NLT

God is so tenderhearted toward you. He desires to spend time with you, to speak to you. So go to Him with your worries. Pour out all the anxious thoughts in your mind. Unburden your heart of all that's concerning you. Tell Him everything that's troubling your spirit and keeping you from focusing on Him.

As you do so, God will come close and listen. Then He will talk to you with a soft voice, pour out His wisdom, and cover you with His love. He will bless you with His peace and presence. Before you know it, you'll find Him transforming your dark valley of despair into a shining gateway of hope.

. . . .

Lord, I feel lost in this dark Valley of Trouble. So I come to You, pouring out my heart. Lead me to the gateway of the hope I have in You!

IN RHYTHM WITH JESUS

*"Come to me. . . . I'll show you how to take a real
rest. . . . Watch how I do it. Learn the unforced
rhythms of grace. . . . Keep company with me
and you'll learn to live freely and lightly."*
MATTHEW 11:28–30 MSG

Worrying is only human, yet it can become an energy-sapper if you don't take your concerns to Jesus on a regular basis. Perhaps you don't want to keep bothering Him with the same old concerns. Or you think you can fix your problems on your own.

Remember that Jesus doesn't want the evil one to steal or destroy your life with worry. Jesus wants you to come to Him, to let Him carry your load. He came so His followers "can have real and eternal life, more and better life than they ever dreamed of" (John 10:10 MSG). So, for a real rest, get away with Jesus. Get into His rhythm. You'll find yourself living not only right but light!

. . . .

*I want to be in rhythm with You, Lord. Let's
spend this moment together.*

YOUR WORRY LIST

*Keep your life free from love of money, and be content
with what you have, for he has said, "I will never
leave you nor forsake you." So we can confidently
say, "The Lord is my helper; I will not fear."*
HEBREWS 13:5–6 ESV

Someone once wrote, "You can tell the size of your God by looking at the size of your worry list. The longer your list, the smaller your God." Hmm. How big is *your* God? How long is *your* worry list?

Do your concerns revolve around money or things you don't really need? Is your discontent rising up because you don't have the latest cell phone, the most fashionable clothes, the best-looking lawn, or the nicest car?

Today consider writing down your worries. See how many things you can cross off, knowing you can be content with what you have. Then hand over to God whatever worries are left, trusting Him, your helper, to provide whatever you truly need.

. . . .

*Lord, help me be content with what I have and trust
You to provide all things I truly do need. Amen.*

REAL LOVE

God showed how much he loved us by sending his one and only Son into the world so that we might have eternal life through him. This is real love— not that we loved God, but that he loved us.

1 JOHN 4:9–10 NLT

Everyone has times when they're feeling unloved, unnoticed, or uncared for—even by the people closest to them! They begin to worry, wondering if they matter at all!

If you're going through such a time, take heart. God loves you more than you can imagine. You're the apple of His eye. He gave up His one and only Son to save you from death and darkness. He loved you even before you loved Him! Although that sounds lopsided, it's true!

God will never *not* love you. He has His eye on you, cares deeply for you. He provides what you need—before you need it!

Rest easy, beloved daughter. Father God's love has you covered!

. . . .

Thank You for loving me, Lord, even when I don't love myself! Fill me with Your love so I can love all those You put in my path.

OPEN DOORS

"Behold, I have set before you an open door, which no one is able to shut. I know that you have but little power, and yet you have kept my word and have not denied my name."
REVELATION 3:8 ESV

Ever worry that you might be on the wrong path? Have you had a door opened or shut in your face lately? No need to worry. As Catherine Wood Marshall wrote, "Often God has to shut a door in our face so that He can subsequently open the door through which He wants us to go."

God has a definite plan for your life. He wants you to be successful, to prosper, to bloom where He's planted you. So instead of worrying if you're on the right or wrong road, go to God. Ask Him to come up behind you and tell you which way to turn, if turn you must. Rest easy, knowing He's guiding you and won't let you go down any rabbit holes.

. . . .

Lord, show me what doors You've opened—or shut.
I'm trusting You to lead me the right way. Amen.

GOD THE REWARDER

*No one can please God without faith. Whoever
goes to God must believe that God exists and
that he rewards those who seek him.*
HEBREWS 11:6 GW

Worry comes when you have a problem or situation that seems unsolvable or hopeless. Or when you're uncertain about how long you can hang on before God will help you or provide an answer.

That's why you must take your worries to God, believing He exists, knowing that because you're seeking His face, He will reward you.

As soon as you enter God's presence and focus on Him, your initial reward is the unsurpassing peace that falls upon you. As you unload your burdens, you realize how small they seem compared to the feats He continually accomplishes and the promises He consistently fulfills. And you now take comfort from the knowledge that God will reward you with an answer to your prayer, a solution to your problem, and strength until they arrive.

. . . .

*I'm seeking Your face before all else, Lord, knowing that
You do exist and You will reward me as I come into Your
presence, beginning with Your unfathomable peace.*

IT'S GOD WHO SAVES

*The LORD said to Gideon, "You have too many
warriors with you. If I let all of you fight the
Midianites, the Israelites will boast to me that they
saved themselves by their own strength."*
JUDGES 7:2 NLT

God told Gideon to gather an army to defeat the Midianites, who'd been raiding Israel. But Gideon had too many warriors with him, so many that the Israelites might imagine their own strength had saved them instead of God.

So, through a series of commands to Gideon, God pared down his army from 32,000 to 300 men, who went on to defeat their enemy.

It's plain to see that when God is in your camp, you need not worry you don't have enough resources to win the day. God will equip you with all the strength, power, and provisions you need— for the victory lies solely in *His* hands!

· ·

*All I need to win the day is to have You on my side, Lord.
You'll provide me with all the strength, power, and provisions
I need because the victory is in Your hands alone!*

A WAY-OUT GOD

*No test or temptation that comes your way is beyond
the course of what others have had to face. All you
need to remember is that God will never let you down;
he'll never let you be pushed past your limit; he'll
always be there to help you come through it.*
1 Corinthians 10:13 msg

No matter what troubles you encounter as you travel through this life, your experiences are really nothing new. Some other woman has walked that road before. So don't worry, fear, or panic. Others have found a way through, and so will you.

Instead of getting caught up in worry, take all your concerns to God. Remember that He'll never let you down. He'll never let things go too far, beyond what you can handle. And He'll stick with you, strengthening and helping you each moment.

So trust God. He'll help you find the perfect escape route while teaching you valuable lessons along the way.

· ·

*Lord, I know others have walked this road before,
so I'm not going to worry. You'll help me find
my way out of this trial, and into You.*

LIKE A CHILD

*But Jesus said, "Let the children come to me.
Don't stop them! For the Kingdom of Heaven
belongs to those who are like these children."*
MATTHEW 19:14 NLT

Little children don't worry. That's because they trust in their parents for everything—food, clothing, water, protection, and love. They're vulnerable and cannot get far without their mother's or father's help and guidance. So they're happy to take their parent's hand, knowing they'll be safely led across the street, through the store, or up the stairs to bed.

That's how God wants you to be—like a trusting child. He wants you not to worry about anything but to rely on Him for everything. He wants you to be humble, realizing your complete dependence on Him, knowing you won't get far without your hand in His.

Be like a child and you'll find yourself growing up securely in God.

· ·

You are such a good father and mother to me, Lord. Help me be like a little child, realizing You'll safely lead me where You'd have me go. I'm putting myself in Your hands. Amen.

EYES ON GOD

We have no might to stand against this great
company that is coming against us. We do not
know what to do, but our eyes are upon You.
2 CHRONICLES 20:12 AMPC

Three armies were coming to attack Jehoshaphat, king of Judah. At first, the king feared for himself and his people, but then he "set himself. . .to seek the Lord" (2 Chronicles 20:3 AMPC)—and prayed.

Jehoshaphat recalled God's strength and power. Then he asked for God's help, admitting that he and his people didn't have the strength to fight that which was coming against them. They didn't know what to do, but their eyes would be on God.

When you don't know what to do, you may worry at first. But prayer will get you realigned with God. Seek Him and recall His strength. Admit your weakness and confusion. Then keep your eyes on God, and you'll gain the victory He provides.

· ·

Lord, You're strong and mighty, and I'm weak.
I don't know what to do, but I'm keeping my eyes
on You, knowing that's where victory lies.

STAND STILL AND SEE

Be not afraid or dismayed at this great multitude; for the battle is not yours, but God's. . . . You shall not need to fight in this battle; take your positions, stand still, and see the deliverance of the Lord [Who is] with you.
2 CHRONICLES 20:15, 17 AMPC

After King Jehoshaphat prayed, God told the king and his people not to worry or be dismayed because the battle before them was God's. All they were to do was to go where God told them to go, stand there, and watch Him save them.

When you come up against a conflict or challenge, keep these powerful verses in mind. They'll alleviate your fears about the situation and your worries about how to handle it.

Then put yourself and your battle in God's hands. Go where He tells you to go. Knowing He's with you, calmly take your stand and watch God work His wonders.

. . . .

*I don't know what You're going to do, Lord,
but I know my role. I'll go where You tell me,
calmly stand there, and watch You work.*

YOUR GREATEST WEAPONS

Jehoshaphat stopped and said, "Listen to me, all you people of Judah and Jerusalem! Believe in the LORD your God, and you will be able to stand firm. Believe in his prophets, and you will succeed."
2 CHRONICLES 20:20 NLT

After God had given King Jehoshaphat his marching orders, he told his people to believe in God, stand firm, and they'd see success in the mighty battle against them. Then he appointed singers to march out *in front of his army* and sing songs of praise to God. "At the very moment they began to sing and give praise, the LORD caused the armies. . .to start fighting among themselves" (2 Chronicles 20:22 NLT). By the time the army of Judah got to the battleground, there was nothing left for them to do but gather up the spoils.

Your greatest weapons against fear and worry are prayer and praise. Pray for guidance, and then praise the God you love and believe in. You'll be able not only to stand strong but to find treasures galore.

. . . .

Lord, thank You for fighting for me. Your faithful love endures forever! (See 2 Chronicles 20:21.)

LOOK UP

Pursue the things over which Christ presides. Don't shuffle along, eyes to the ground, absorbed with the things right in front of you. Look up, and be alert to what is going on around Christ—that's where the action is. See things from his perspective.
COLOSSIANS 3:2 MSG

Have you ever seen people walking along, looking down at their cell phones? They're so worried they're going to miss the latest text, email, or news bite, so absorbed in what's happening on their mobile device that they aren't watching where they're going. And before they know it, they've either walked into something or fallen into a hole and hurt themselves.

God wants your focus off the ground and on to heavenly things. He wants you checking out what Jesus is doing, seeing things from His point of view. Looking up at Him will keep you from stumbling where God wants you soaring.

. . . .

Jesus, I get so attached to things of this earth—and that's when I stumble into worry. Help me keep my eyes looking up to You, alert to what You're doing.

COME AS YOU ARE

*Let everyone come who is thirsty [who is painfully
conscious of his need of those things by which the
soul is refreshed, supported, and strengthened];
and whoever [earnestly] desires to do it, let him
come. . .and drink the water of Life without cost.*
REVELATION 22:17 AMPC

Have you worried you aren't good enough to come to God and
unload your cares and concerns? That you aren't worthy enough
to ask for and receive God's mercy, Jesus' love, and the Holy
Spirit's help?

In the hymn "Come Ye Sinners," lyricist Joseph Hart provides
these words: "Come, ye weary, heavy-laden/Lost and ruined by
the fall/If you tarry 'til you're better/You will never come at all."

God knows you aren't perfect. That's why He sent Jesus to
save you and left the Holy Spirit to help you. So don't tarry. Go
to God and set your burdens down. Take up His light, and you'll
find refreshment for your soul, strength for your spirit, and love
for your heart.

. . . .

*I'm coming to You just as I am, Lord.
Take my worries and give me Your peace.*

SPIRITUAL SOWING

He who sows to his own flesh (lower nature, sensuality) will from the flesh reap decay and ruin and destruction, but he who sows to the Spirit will from the Spirit reap eternal life.
GALATIANS 6:8 AMPC

When you're in a state of worry, you're sowing to your flesh, planting worry-seeds that will reap only more worry, or worse, grow into outright fear and panic. Before you know it, you're doing or saying something you didn't want to do or say that may destroy or deaden the spirits of others.

So, when worry crops up, do yourself and the world a favor. Take some deep breaths. Dig into the Word. Find a verse that calms your spirit and builds up your faith. Write that verse upon your heart. Then seek God's face and peace. Soon, you'll be sowing in the Spirit and reaping the light of eternal life.

. . . .

*I'm tired of sowing worry, Lord. It only grows up
into bigger worries, or worse. Help me grow in
You, sowing to the Spirit, reaping Your light.*

BEING A BLESSING

*We can't allow ourselves to get tired of living the right way.
Certainly, each of us will receive everlasting life at the
proper time, if we don't give up. Whenever we have the
opportunity, we have to do what is good for everyone.*
GALATIANS 6:9–10 GW

If you allow yourself to be bogged down by worry, you won't have the energy to focus on anything but those things that concern and affect you. With your eyes on only yourself, you can no longer take advantage of—or even *see*—opportunities to help someone else. You stop being a blessing to others.

God wants you to love not just Him and yourself but your neighbors: the people lying by the road, wounded and bleeding physically, emotionally, spiritually, financially, and mentally.

Today, get out of yourself and into God and others by doing something good for your neighbor, friend, relative, or a stranger. As soon as you start focusing on others, your worries will fade in the light of love.

· ·

*I want to expand my vision, Lord, to help those in need.
Show me who I can help and love in Your name.*

GOD'S PATIENCE

The Lord isn't slow to do what he promised. . . . Rather, he is patient for your sake. He doesn't want to destroy anyone but wants all people to have an opportunity to turn to him and change the way they think and act.
2 PETER 3:9 GW

Many women come to church alone because their mates don't yet believe in Jesus. Some people call these women "church widows." Perhaps you're one of them. You worry and wonder, *Will my loved one ever believe?*

It's good to be concerned about the salvation of others, but it shouldn't be all consuming. Instead of spending your time worrying about your loved ones—whether they are spouses, children, parents, or friends—fix your eyes on God. He has tons of patience *and* He has a plan, wanting to give everyone the opportunity to follow His Son. In the meantime, be the best God-follower you can be. And pray for the souls of others, leaving their fate in God's capable hands.

. . . .

Lord, thank You for always being with me. Today, I lift up the following pre-Christians to You. . .

GOD MAKES YOUR PATHS PLAIN

Trust in the LORD with all your heart, and do not lean on your own understanding. In all your ways acknowledge him, and he will make straight your paths.
PROVERBS 3:5–6 ESV

At some point in your life, chances are you asked God to tell you what He would have you do to serve Him, whether as a missionary, pastor, wife, mother, writer, secretary, company executive, mayor, and so on. And He answered your prayer, directing you into an area that you already had a passion for. But then, as the years passed, your passion ebbed a bit, and now you're wondering if there is some new road He wants you to take. Or you're worrying that maybe you had it wrong from the very beginning!

Perhaps it's time to ask God again to show you which way to go. Then trust Him to do so—but don't make a move until He's made everything plain. Patience will be your reward.

. . . .

I'm leaning into and on You, Lord. Show me the road You want me on. I'm trusting in You.

STAND STILL AND CONSIDER

*Hear this. . .stand still and consider
the wondrous works of God.*
JOB 37:14 AMPC

Today consider taking a break from the hectic pace of your life and going for a relaxing prayer walk. Head out into nature, whether that is your backyard, a nearby park, a beach, a creek, or a tree planted in the city sidewalk. Once there, stand still and think about all the wonderful things God has created for your provision and enjoyment.

Touch the bark on a tree or the petal of a flower. If it's warm enough, take off your shoes and stick your feet in the grass or wiggle your toes in the sand. Look up into the heavens and take in the awesomeness of God.

As you prayerfully reconnect with God's creation and consider its vastness, your worries will seem trivial, and your lips and mind will be filled with nothing but praise.

. . . .

*I'm overwhelmed with the variety and vastness of all You
have created, Lord. Help me stop worrying and start admiring
all You've done for those You love in heaven and on earth.*

SUPERHUMAN POWER

When you received the message of God. . .you
welcomed it not as the word of [mere] men, but as it
truly is, the Word of God, which is effectually at work
in you who believe [exercising its superhuman power
in those who adhere to and trust in and rely on it].
1 THESSALONIANS 2:13 AMPC

Imagine it! God's Word is working in you, "exercising its *super-human* power" within you as you live it out, trusting in and relying on it!

God's Word is everything you need! It saves, guides, warns, rewards, and counsels you. It trains you up into the woman God has created you to be. It revives your spirit, restores your strength, comforts your heart, nourishes your soul, and renews your mind. It strengthens you, gives you joy, and prospers you.

Forget about the worries. Focus on the Word. And God will change you from the inside out!

. . . .

I want to tap into Your superhuman power, Lord. Take my
worries into Your hands and pour out Your Word upon me!

SERVING GOD AT SUCH A TIME

*"And who knows whether you have not come
to the kingdom for such a time as this?"*
ESTHER 4:14 ESV

Esther, a beautiful Jewish girl, was an orphan who became a queen. Then, when her cousin Mordecai discovered the Jews were being persecuted, he sent word to Esther, telling her that this may be her time to talk to the king and ask for his help to save her people.

After receiving his message, a resolved Esther told Mordecai to ask her people to fast and pray for three days, saying, "Then I will go to the king, though it is against the law, and if I perish, I perish" (Esther 4:16 ESV).

Perhaps you feel God is calling you, willing you to be brave in His name. If so, pray. Ask God to replace your worries with His peace, your fears with His courage. Don't miss this opportunity to serve God at such a time as this.

. . . .

*Lord, reveal to me any opportunities You have for me.
Fortified by Your peace and courage, I will serve You.*

MEDITATE ON WONDERS

Every day [with its new reasons] will I bless You
[affectionately and gratefully praise You]; yes, I will praise
Your name forever and ever. . . . On the glorious splendor of
Your majesty and on Your wondrous works I will meditate.
PSALM 145:2, 5 AMPC

David, the shepherd boy who turned king, loved to talk to God. Many of his psalms speak of his fears, woes, and worries. But David also looked for the good in his life. He actively kept his eyes open for the new and amazing things the Lord was doing every day and praised God for them. Then he would keep God's wonders in mind all day long.

Why not follow David's example? After unloading your worries, actively seek something new to praise God for. Keep your eyes open to His wonders and works around you. Think about them throughout your day. You'll find yourself so busy looking for the good, you won't have time to worry.

· ·

Today I'm looking for new reasons to praise and adore
You, Lord! On Your works and wonders I will meditate!

LISTENING TO WISDOM

*Whoso hearkens to me [Wisdom] shall dwell
securely and in confident trust and shall be
quiet, without fear or dread of evil.*
PROVERBS 1:33 AMPC

No matter what Bible version you have, the verse above speaks volumes. God's Word puts it this way, "Whoever listens to me will live without worry and will be free from the dread of disaster." The "me" here is Wisdom, who, in some chapters of Proverbs, is personified as a woman.

If you want to live without worry, you need to not just pour out your troubles to God but to *listen* to Him when He responds. To follow where His words and voice lead. When you do, you will be free not only from fretting but actually from the fear of evil and disaster. You will no longer find yourself mentally envisioning the worst-case scenario and rehearsing your reaction to it but living securely, quietly, and peacefully, confident that God will give you the *best*-case scenario.

. . . .

*I want to live in quiet confidence. My ears
are open to Your wisdom, Lord. Speak!*

THAT SPECIAL GLOW

"If you are generous with the hungry and start giving yourselves to the down-and-out, your lives will begin to glow in the darkness, your shadowed lives will be bathed in sunlight."
Isaiah 58:10 MSG

When your worries become a shadow in your life, get out of yourself and into others. Find a food pantry you can donate to. Consider volunteering at the next Thanksgiving meal at a local soup kitchen. Weed a widow's garden, offer to drive a carless person to church, or help support a child who lives in poverty.

As you expend your energy to help others, you will begin to glow in this dark world. Your shadowed life will be bathed in God's Son's light. And you'll find people saying, "I want what she has." There's no better witness than that.

. . . .

Lord, I want to get out from underneath this shadow of worry. Open my eyes to the needs around me. What can I do today to help someone, become a powerful force in Your kingdom, and brighten up my own life—all at the same time?

FAITH OVER FRET

*"I'm convinced: You can do anything and everything.
Nothing and no one can upset your plans."*
JOB 42:2 MSG

God has made you certain promises. You can find them in His Word. But to those promises you need to add your faith. You must be convinced that God can and will do anything and everything, that no one can mess up His plans for you and the rest of His creation. When you have such certainty, your faith will win over your fretting every time!

To shore up such faith that God's Word trumps your worries, remember what He said in Isaiah 55:11 (MSG): "The words that come out of my mouth [will] not come back empty-handed. They'll do the work I sent them to do, they'll complete the assignment I gave them."

Don't worry. God promises to make good on His promises. You have His word on it!

. . . .

*Help me shore up my faith, Lord. Show me how to grow
in certainty that You will do what You've promised to do
in my life. That no one can mess up Your plans for me!*

NEW HOPE EVERY MORNING

There's one other thing I remember, and remembering, I keep a grip on hope: GOD's loyal love couldn't have run out, his merciful love couldn't have dried up. They're created new every morning. How great your faithfulness!
LAMENTATIONS 3:21–22 MSG

You may find that some wounds seem harder to heal than others or that some of the same worries keep cropping up.

Take heart. Keep your grip on hope by remembering that God's love and mercy never run out or dry up. Every morning Your Creator has a new supply that you can access through spending time in His Word, praying, and meditating. Just give God room and time to speak through the Spirit. Open yourself to some new thoughts. God, in His faithfulness, will meet you just where you need Him the most.

. . . .

Lord, in times of doubt, trial, and worry, remind me that You are always there for me with a new supply of love and mercy every morning. Speak deep into my heart. And I will praise Your never-ending faithfulness to me!

ROCK ON IN GOD'S TRUTH

For in the day of trouble He will hide me in His shelter; in the secret place of His tent will He hide me; He will set me high upon a rock.
PSALM 27:5 AMPC

When you are filled with worries, torn up by troubles, there's only one place to go: to God in prayer. Run to Him. Meld your spirit with His Spirit. Feel Jesus' love and compassion. Let your worries slip off of you and onto Him.

See yourself as hiding in the shelter of God's love. God pulls you up and sets you upon the rock, high above your earthly cares, all the problems, dangers, and trials that want to drag you down.

As you stand upon the rock, God whispers His encouragement, reminding you that you're a strong Christian woman, a sister of Jesus, a beloved daughter of a King, and a conduit of God's Spirit. Rock on in His truth!

. . . .

I'm running to You, Lord. Hide me in Your secret place. Lift me up to the rock. Remind me who I am in You!

GOD RAINS BLESSINGS

Blessed be the Lord, the God of Israel, Who has fulfilled with His hands what He promised with His mouth.
2 CHRONICLES 6:4 AMPC

The land was experiencing a great famine when the Lord said to the prophet Elijah, "Go, show yourself to Ahab, and I will send rain upon the earth" (1 Kings 18:1 AMPC). Elijah followed God's command and eventually said to King Ahab, "Go up, eat and drink, for there is the sound of abundance of rain" (1 Kings 18:41 AMPC). Then Elijah went to the top of Mount Carmel, bowed down to the ground, and put his face between his knees.

Six times Elijah told his servant to go and look toward the sea. And each time the servant came back, saying he'd seen nothing. But the seventh time, he saw a cloud that was followed by torrential rains.

Don't let worry and frustration cloud your wonder at what God has said He'll do. Just keep looking. God will do "with His hands what He promised with His mouth."

. . . .

I'm believing in Your promise to me, Lord.
I know You'll rain down Your blessing!

SWEET-SMELLING INCENSE

Is anyone crying for help? God is
listening, ready to rescue you.
PSALM 34:17 MSG

Do you sometimes wonder if God is listening to you? Do you worry your prayers are falling on deaf ears?

Don't. It's the evil one who wants you to think God neither hears nor cares about your worries, problems, and questions. It's the father of lies' aim to drive a wedge between you and the Lord. Yet the truth is that every word you utter in prayer rises up to God like sweet-smelling incense (see Revelation 8:4).

As you go to God in prayer today, imagine Him eagerly waiting to hear what you have to say. See Him hanging on every word. Then take the time to listen to His response. His words will rescue you, bringing you ever closer to Him.

· ·

"God, come close. Come quickly! Open your ears—
it's my voice you're hearing! Treat my prayer as
sweet incense rising; my raised hands are my
evening prayers" (Psalm 141:1–2 MSG).

WORDLESS PRAYERS

Likewise the Spirit helps us in our weakness. For we do not know what to pray for as we ought, but the Spirit himself intercedes for us with groanings too deep for words.

ROMANS 8:26 ESV

Sometimes your worries and troubles may be so burdensome that you find yourself not knowing how to put your pleas to God into words. That's where the Holy Spirit comes in. He knows just what your heart, soul, mind, and spirit are trying to express and delivers your yearnings to God.

C. S. Lewis wrote that one of his rules about prayer is "to pray without words when I am able, but to fall back on words when tired or otherwise below par."*

The point is never to avoid prayer because you don't know how to put your petitions into words. Just go to God as you are. Sit before Him, allowing Him to enter in. Raise your spirit to His, and all things will be made clear—for you and for God.

. . . .

I'm coming to You, Lord, for a spirit-to-Spirit talk, resting in Your presence, knowing You will understand all that lies within me. Amen.

*C. S. Lewis, *The Collected Letters of C. S. Lewis, Volume III: Narnia, Cambridge, and Joy 1950–1963.* Copyright © 2007 by C. S. Lewis Pte. Ltd. All rights reserved. Used with permission of HarperCollins Publishers. *Yours, Jack: Spiritual Direction from C. S. Lewis.* Copyright © 2008 by C. S. Lewis Pte. Ltd. All rights reserved. Used with permission of HarperCollins Publishers.

THE REALITY OF FAITH

Now faith is the assurance (the confirmation, the title deed) of the things [we] hope for, being the proof of things [we] do not see and the conviction of their reality [faith perceiving as real fact what is not revealed to the senses].
HEBREWS 11:1 AMPC

Worry is often prompted by fear, which some people say stands for False Evidence Appearing Real. Yet God would have you overcome those worries and fears with faith in Him and His Word. Faith is not wishful thinking but *knowing* God has made certain promises to you and that He will keep those promises. So you can accept them as your present reality even if you do not yet perceive them.

As you read the Bible, you begin to see and understand that all God has said and promised came to pass for those who believed. And this same fact holds true for you today. So let go of fears and worries, and hang on to faith and hope. God is already working on your behalf, transforming His promises into your reality even as you read these words.

· ·

I believe, Lord. I believe.

BOLDLY BELIEVING

If you don't know what you're doing, pray to
the Father. He loves to help. You'll get his help,
and won't be condescended to when you ask for it.
Ask boldly, believingly, without a second thought.
JAMES 1:5 MSG

God loves bold prayers—people who come to Him believing, who have no doubt in their mind that God will give them the wisdom and help they need just when they need it.

In this chapter, James (Jesus' brother) goes on to talk about those who doubt, writing, "People who 'worry their prayers' are like wind-whipped waves. Don't think you're going to get anything from the Master that way, adrift at sea, keeping all your options open" (James 1:6–8 MSG). In other words, God delights in people who boldly come to Him in faith, holding no doubt in their minds.

Ask and believe, and you will receive all the guidance and help you need from the Master, trusting Him more than your world or your own abilities.

. . . .

Lord, I'm trusting You—and only You—for the
help and wisdom I need. Show me the way.

WORDS OF LIFE

*Remember what you said to me, your servant—I hang
on to these words for dear life! These words hold me
up in bad times; yes, your promises rejuvenate me.*
PSALM 119:49–50 MSG

When you're going through a hard time, burdened by worries, there is only one place where you can find comfort: God's Word. It is there alone that you'll find your strength, nourishment, comfort, and hope.

If you're so troubled and worried that you can't even think, the best Bible book to go to is Psalms. It's like reading someone's personal journal. The psalmists write of their troubles, fears, doubts, worries, and hardships. Yet they find reasons to praise God for all the wonderful things He is doing and has done in the past and they are certain He will do in the future.

Hang on to God's words. They will speak to your heart, lift your spirit, and soothe your soul.

· ·

*Dear God, I long for Your comfort. Show me in Your
Word what You would have me read, know, and
study. Hold me up with Your precious words!*

LOOKING TO JESUS

Let us strip off and throw aside every encumbrance (unnecessary weight) and that sin which so readily (deftly and cleverly) clings to and entangles us, and let us run with patient endurance and steady and active persistence the appointed course of the race that is set before us, looking away [from all that will distract] to Jesus.
HEBREWS 12:1–2 AMPC

Although today's verse seems extraordinarily long, it gets right to the heart of the matter of worry and what to do about it.

Many faith-walkers that have gone before you have proven the truth of God. Their example should be enough to prompt you to strip off worry and anything else that hinders your own walk in Christ. View worry as just a distraction, something that keeps you from living in God's light and truth. And see Jesus as your focal point—in life and in prayer.

Jesus, thank You for not just saving me from death but from the fears and worries that dog womankind. Help me keep my eyes on You alone and walk Your way in truth.

FELLOW WORRIERS

*Peace I leave with you; My [own] peace I now give
and bequeath to you. Not as the world gives do
I give to you. Do not let your hearts be troubled,
neither let them be afraid. [Stop allowing yourselves
to be agitated and disturbed. . .and unsettled.]*
JOHN 14:27 AMPC

Lately you've found yourself in a pretty good place, each day dutifully handing your worries over to God and tapping into Jesus' peace through prayer. But then someone comes along venting his or her own worries. Before you know it, the worries you thought you'd left behind are rearing up all over again. What's a woman to do?

Be a good listener, but don't let someone else's fears trigger your own. Simply pray for your fellow worrier with the realization that his or her worries are what they see as truth. But you know better. For *your* truth lies in the Word of Life. You have Jesus to give you the peace you need and the wisdom to know that, in God, all is truly well.

. . . .

With You, Jesus, I'm a fellow warrior not a worrier!

A GREAT CALM

*And He arose and rebuked the wind and said to the sea,
Hush now! Be still (muzzled)! And the wind ceased (sank
to rest as if exhausted by its beating) and there was
[immediately] a great calm (a perfect peacefulness).*
MARK 4:39–40 AMPC

Jesus suggested He and the disciples take the boats to the other side of the lake. On the way, Jesus fell asleep in the stern even after a huge storm rose up and water started filling the boats!

So the disciples woke Jesus, saying, "Don't you care if we're about to die?" That's when Jesus got up, calmed the storm, and then asked the disciples, "Where is your faith?"

When worries start to flood into your life, allow faith to anchor you. Remind yourself of Jesus' love and power and of the words of Minister Lloyd John Ogilvie, who said, "Sometimes the Lord rides out the storm with us and other times He calms the restless sea around us. Most of all, He calms the storm inside us in our deepest inner soul."

. . . .

Lord, calm the storm deep within me.

GOOD SPIRITUALITY

*Be happy [in your faith] and rejoice and be glad-hearted
continually (always); be unceasing in prayer [praying
perseveringly]; thank [God] in everything [no matter
what the circumstances may be, be thankful and
give thanks], for this is the will of God for you.*
1 THESSALONIANS 5:16–18 AMPC

Inventor William Painter said, "Saying thank you is more than
good manners. It is good spirituality." The apostle Paul, author
of Thessalonians, is in complete agreement.

Instead of worrying, God wants you to rejoice continually, to
pray without ceasing, and to thank God for everything—"no matter
what the circumstances may be." That may sound like a really
tall order, but if that's what God wants and wills you to do, He'll
give you the power and strength to do it! Besides, if you begin
to spend all your time rejoicing, praying, and thanking God, you
won't have time to worry!

. . . .

*Help me, Lord, to seek constant joy in You. To pray
continually, giving You my worries as soon as they
creep into my mind then leaving them in Your hands.
I thank You no matter what happens or when!*

REGAINING A FOOTHOLD OF FAITH

*When I said, "My feet are slipping," your mercy, O
LORD, continued to hold me up. When I worried about
many things, your assuring words soothed my soul.*
PSALM 94:18–19 GW

When you start to slip into worrying, when your feet of faith start
to lose their purchase, tell God all about it. Acknowledge to
yourself that His kindness and compassion *will* help you regain
a foothold. Allow His words to soothe your soul and nurture
your spirit.

No matter when worry, trouble, or danger strikes, God is right
there with you in the midst of things. He promises He'll never
leave your side.

Norman Vincent Peale wrote, "Frequently remind yourself
that God is with you, that He will never fail you, that you can
count upon Him. Say these words, 'God is with me, helping me.'"
As you say these words, envision God right next to you, and your
faith will prevail.

. . . .

*Lord, thank You for always being there when I need You, loving
me, holding me up, helping me out, and soothing my soul.*

KNOWING GOD

"Give your entire attention to what God is doing right now, and don't get worked up about what may or may not happen tomorrow. God will help you deal with whatever hard things come up when the time comes."
MATTHEW 6:34 MSG

The human imagination has a way of leading you astray by coming up with a myriad of different scenarios that may or may not become your reality. But Jesus says a believer's attention should be focused on God and where He's working today, in this moment, not on tomorrow and its uncertainties, knowing God will help with whatever happens when it happens.

But how do you get there from here? Move closer to God. Learn all you can about Him. Know Him. And your worries about tomorrow will flee.

Author Corrie ten Boom said, "Never be afraid to trust an unknown future to a known God." Wise words for today's—and tomorrow's—woman.

. . . .

Help me, Lord, to keep my focus on You and what You're doing right now. I'm trusting my unknown future to You, the God I know and love.

REFUGE, SHIELD, HOPE, AND PEACE

You are my refuge and my shield; your word is my source of hope. . . . Those who love your instructions have great peace and do not stumble.
PSALM 119:114, 165 NLT

When you're worried, lost, and confused, when you don't know where to go or who to turn to, go to God and open His Word. There you will find the refuge you so desperately seek, the safety you need, the hope you thirst for, and the compass you crave.

You can run to God no matter where you are for He is as near to you as your breath. Within His presence and power, you will be shielded. There you can wait until you have gained His wisdom and peace, until you know what to say or do. God will speak into your heart. He will make sure you do not stumble as you follow His instructions and take the next steps.

. . . .

Thank You, Lord, for being my constant refuge, shield, and hope. In Your Word alone do I find wisdom and peace.

THE OPENER OF EYES, HEARTS, AND THE WORD

"Did not our hearts burn within us while he talked to us on the road, while he opened to us the Scriptures?"
LUKE 24:32 ESV

After Jesus' death, two of His disciples, confused and sorrowful, headed to Emmaus and talked about what had happened. As they were walking, Jesus joined them, yet they did not recognize Him. Hearing their story about Him, Jesus "interpreted to them in all the Scriptures the things concerning himself" (Luke 24:27 ESV). Later, when He broke bread with them, "their eyes were opened" (Luke 24:31 ESV), and Jesus vanished. It was then they realized why their hearts had burned within them as He'd spoken to them.

Like those disciples, at times you may feel confused, alone, and worried about what has happened or will happen. But you can take heart, because Jesus comes alongside to explain things to you. He'll give you hope—for He still walks and talks with you!

. . . .

Jesus, sometimes I feel all alone. Help me to recognize Your presence walking with me. Open my eyes and heart as I seek Your Word.

GOD'S ARM

*Be the arm [of Your servants—their strength and defense]
every morning, our salvation in the time of trouble.*
Isaiah 33:2 AMPC

Author E. M. Bounds wrote, "If God is not first in our thoughts and efforts in the morning, he will be in the last place the remainder of the day." The Bible says King David sought God's guidance through early morning prayer (see Psalm 143:8). Even Jesus, long before the sun rose, went out alone to a deserted place and prayed to God (see Mark 1:35).

It's obvious that starting your day with prayer, seeking to make God your primary guide and focus instead of your own self, sets you on the right course. Before you're out the door, you'll be armed with God's strength, protection, and saving power. The volume of His voice in your heart, mind, and soul will then rise above all other sounds and whistles, keeping your feet on the right path and worries and other distractors at bay (see Isaiah 33:3).

. . . .

Lord, be my strength and defense every morning.

WISDOM OVER WORRY

Listen well to my words; tune your ears to my voice.
Keep my message in plain view at all times. Concentrate!
Learn it by heart! Those who discover these words live,
really live; body and soul, they're bursting with health.
PROVERBS 4:20–22 MSG

David writes that worrying leads to evil and harm (see Psalm 37:8). His son Solomon tells you God's wisdom leads to an awesome life. So if you want to have the best life, dig into God's wisdom. You'll find it throughout the Bible but especially in Proverbs. There King Solomon provides insight into how to deal with everyday issues, including how to work, act, talk, think, curb your anger, and so much more.

In the verses above, Solomon strongly suggests you learn some verses by heart. Perhaps you could start by reading Proverbs every day. When you come to a verse that really speaks to you, that gives you guidance or peace about a situation, memorize it. Before you know it, God's wisdom will stand in place of your worry.

. . . .

I want to live a good life, Lord. Help me
replace my worry with Your Word!

WARDING OFF WORRIES

*O L*ORD *God, my savior, I cry out to you during the
day and at night. Let my prayer come into your
presence. Turn your ear to hear my cries.*
P*SALM* 88:1–2 GW

Cynthia Lewis says, "If your day is hemmed in with prayer, it is less likely to come unraveled." Let's take that a step further and say that if your day is hemmed in with prayer, *you're* less likely to come unraveled!

Chances are you brush your teeth in the morning and again in the evening. You were taught to do this as a child and now do it automatically, without even thinking. And that's a good thing, for brushing teeth helps ward off cavities.

So why not start the practice of praying in the morning and then again in the evening. As you do this day after day, it too will become something you do automatically. And it'll be a good thing because doing so will help ward off worries, giving you a focused mind by day and a restful one at night!

· ·

*Lord, let my prayer come into Your
loving presence day and night.*

GOD ONLY KNOWS

For the Lord sees not as man sees; for man looks on the outward appearance, but the Lord looks on the heart.
1 SAMUEL 16:7 AMPC

Everybody wants to be liked. It's only natural. Yet problems may arise when you assume you *know* what someone else is thinking about you or your ideas, comments, and suggestions, and you begin to worry about what you do to please him or her.

Although people can give you clues—through expression, voice, body language, attitude, or demeanor—as to how they think or feel about you—only God can truly see within peoples' hearts and minds to know what they're really thinking (see 1 Kings 8:39; John 2:24–25; Matthew 9:4).

God doesn't want you to worry about the opinions or thoughts of others or to let them hold you back from what He's calling you to do or say. Your job is to please Him alone (see 1 Thessalonians 2:4). He'll take care of the rest.

· ·

Help me, Lord, to not worry about what others may think about me but to live and serve You alone!

THE PEACE OF GOD'S KINGDOM

*Now may the Lord of peace Himself grant you His peace
(the peace of His kingdom) at all times and in all ways
[under all circumstances and conditions, whatever comes].*
2 THESSALONIANS 3:16 AMPC

The philosopher Michel de Montaigne, who lived in the 1500s, said: "My life has been filled with terrible misfortune; most of which never happened." Chances are that if you looked closely at your own life, you'd agree.

And there are modern-day statistics to back up Montaigne's statement. A recent study says 40 percent of the things you worry about will never happen; 30 percent are in the past, which you can't change; 12 percent are needless worries about your health; and 10 percent are trivial worries that fall into the miscellaneous category. That leaves you with 8 percent of worries that have actual substance in your life.

So tell your worries to hit the road, and walk in God's path of peace.

. . . .

*Lord of peace, fill me with Your presence and the peace of
Your kingdom at all times and in all ways, whatever comes.*

ALWAYS THERE

*Even if my father and mother abandon
me, the L*ORD *will hold me close.*
PSALM 27:10 NLT

Relationships with others can be difficult at times. Through some misunderstanding or deliberate affront, some family members can become estranged. Others may find themselves divorced. Even friends can fade away. And then, of course, some loved ones are lost through death.

Yet there's no need to worry about being alone. Even if your mother and father abandon you, God will always be there to hold you close. For He, your eternal and loving Father, promises to take you in and care for you. And His Son, your friend Jesus, will stick closer to you than a brother (see Proverbs 18:24).

When you feel as if you're all alone—even when in a crowded room—don't worry. Go to God. Revel in His presence. Feel His light and love within. He will never leave you to go it alone.

*Thank You, Lord, for being the love and light
that's forever with me—from beginning to end.
Hold me close as I lie in Your arms.*

MOMENT BY MOMENT

Whatever you do, put your whole heart and soul into it,
as into work done for God, and not merely for men—
knowing that your real reward, a heavenly one, will come
from God, since you are actually employed by Christ.
COLOSSIANS 3:23–24 PHILLIPS

Are you living in the future or in the present moment?

In his book *The Weight of Glory*, C. S. Lewis writes, "Happy work is best done by the man who takes his long-term plans somewhat lightly and works from moment to moment 'as to the Lord.' It is only our daily bread that we are encouraged to ask for. The present is the only time in which any duty can be done or any grace received."*

When worry begins to creep into your day, check to see where you're living. If it's in the future, take a step back. Then ask God to draw you into the present moment. He'll get you back on course.

. . . .

Lord, help me stay living in the present moment,
where You and my peace reside.

GIVE GOD A CALL

For you, O Lord, are good and forgiving, abounding in steadfast love to all who call upon you. Give ear, O LORD, to my prayer; listen to my plea for grace. In the day of my trouble I call upon you, for you answer me.
PSALM 86:5–7 ESV

No one is perfect—except God of course. But you're a mere human. You're bound to make a few mistakes. There will probably be times when you wrong yourself, God, or a fellow human being. Before you realize it, you're caught in a whirl of worry—about the effects of your misstep, what God and others may be thinking about you (and your words and actions), how or what you'll say when you ask for forgiveness, and so on.

To break free of this whirl of worry, call on God. Remind yourself how forgiving He is, how much He loves you. Ask Him to hear your prayer and to bestow His forgiveness, and then expect His answer.

. . . .

Lord, I'm calling on You, counting on Your love and forgiveness. Hear my prayer. Tell me how to handle this situation.

WELL EMPLOYED

Study this Book of Instruction continually. Meditate on it day and night so you will be sure to obey everything written in it. Only then will you prosper and succeed in all you do.
JOSHUA 1:8 NLT

Unlike worry, meditation will help you prosper and succeed! You may find it hard to pull yourself out of the world and into God. Fortunately, those who've gone before are here to help. About meditation, St. Francis advises:

If the heart wanders or is distracted, bring it back to the point quite gently and replace it tenderly in its Master's presence. And even if you did nothing during the whole of your hour but bring your heart back and place it again in our Lord's presence, though it went away every time you brought it back, your hour will be very well employed.

If you're new to meditation, begin with five minutes a day, and then build up to ten. You'll soon find the peace you crave.

. . . .

"May the words of my mouth and the meditation of my heart be pleasing to you, O LORD" (Psalm 19:14 NLT).

UNFAMILIAR PATHS

I will lead the blind on unfamiliar roads. I will lead them on unfamiliar paths. I will turn darkness into light in front of them. I will make rough places smooth. These are the things I will do for them, and I will never abandon them.

Isaiah 42:16 GW

Worrying about what may happen in the future, what to do in the present, or how to get over the past can make you feel as if you're blind, walking in the dark, lost and confused. Yet you need not worry about stumbling in the dark, unable to see the road ahead of you because God promises to lead you down unfamiliar paths. In fact, He'll transform the darkness into light right in front of your eyes! He'll make rocky places smooth. And He will never abandon you.

Because God promises that He'll always be with you, you can cease your worry and say with author Mary Gardiner Brainard, "I would rather walk with God in the dark than go alone in the light."

. . . .

I'm with You, Lord, all the way! Lead me down Your path, into Your light!

GOD ONE STEP AHEAD

"I will answer them before they even call to me.
While they are still talking about their needs,
I will go ahead and answer their prayers!"
Isaiah 65:24 NLT

How wonderful to have a God that answers you before you even cry out for Him! That while you're busy pouring out your worries, presenting God your what-if scenarios, and trying to put words to all you feel and are concerned about, He is already answering your petitions!

That's just who God is! That's just how much He cares about you! If you memorize today's verse and truly believe it, you can break up whatever worries come your way. You will trust the One who answers before you speak, the One who sees all the concerns, problems, and heartaches and is ready to soothe, solve, and salve.

. . . .

Lord, I'm taking up my shield of faith in You, knowing that You are already going before me, answering my prayer, solving my problem, and healing my heart. I praise Your name!

LIVING CAREFREE

So be content with who you are, and don't put on airs.
God's strong hand is on you; he'll promote you at the right
time. Live carefree before God; he is most careful with you.
1 PETER 5:6–7 MSG

God doesn't want you worrying about the who, what, when, where, how, and why in your life. He doesn't want you to be unhappy where you are right now, in this moment. He wants you to totally trust Him, to know and believe He has a plan for your life—and it's so much better than anything you ever dreamed or imagined.

The same strong hand God used to part the waters and lead the Israelites out of Egypt and into the Promised Land is the same hand that is now upon you.

Trust God's timing. Live without care before Him by handing all your worries over to Him. You're His precious cargo. He's cradling you, loving you, protecting you. Just rest and relax in Him.

· ·

Take my worries, Lord. Then hold me until I can feel
Your peace, love, and strong hand upon me.

MAKE UP YOUR MIND

I have cheerfully made up my mind to be proud of my weaknesses, because they mean a deeper experience of the power of Christ. I can even enjoy weaknesses, suffering, privations, persecutions and difficulties for Christ's sake. For my very weakness makes me strong in him.
2 CORINTHIANS 12:10 PHILLIPS

God gives many gifts to His faithful followers, one of which is that no matter how weak you are, no matter how much you suffer or how often you worry, your very weaknesses give Christ the chance to shine through you. For this formula to work, though, you must have faith and then make up your mind to live it.

God moves when you're truly helpless. He provides when you have no more resources left. He will give you the power to overcome all things—even worry. So revel in God, thanking Him no matter what comes. He has all the strength you need to triumph—to His glory!

. . . .

I've made up my mind, Lord! I'm going to be content no matter what! In You I have the strength to endure all!

GOD MEETS YOUR NEEDS

The Lord is my Shepherd [to feed, guide, and shield me],
I shall not lack. He makes me lie down in [fresh, tender] green
pastures; He leads me beside the still and restful waters.
PSALM 23:1–2 AMPC

In 1943, Abraham Maslow proposed a theory in psychology called Maslow's hierarchy of needs. He explained that there are five levels of human needs. The first level, which is physiological—food, water, warmth, and rest—must be satisfied before individuals can take care of needs higher up.

Amazingly enough, those are the *same* needs David covers in the first two verses of Psalm 23! David says he doesn't want for anything because God is his Shepherd who feeds, guides, and shields him. He makes David lie down and rest. He leads David to water.

So there's no "need" to worry about how your needs will be met. God will take care of everything! Why? Because He's not just any shepherd—He's the *Great* Shepherd!

. . . .

Knowing that You will meet all my needs is a load off my
mind, Lord. Thank You for being my Great Shepherd!

GOD WALKS WITH YOU

*Yes, though I walk through the [deep, sunless]
valley of the shadow of death, I will fear or dread
no evil, for You are with me; Your rod [to protect]
and Your staff [to guide], they comfort me.*
PSALM 23:4 AMPC

God not only satisfies your basic human needs for food, water, warmth, and rest but also walks with you, equipped with two tools to make sure you're safe and heading the right way. He uses the first tool, His shepherd's rod, to stave off any force, power, or evil that threatens your life. He uses the second, His staff, to guide you through the shadows and onto the right path.

So the next time you're worried about your safety or where to take your next step, pray to God—the all-powerful Father and Shepherd who loves and adores you—remembering He's well equipped to protect you and more than ready to guide you.

. . . .

*Lord, I feel Your presence by my side.
With You walking alongside me, I know I'll
be safe and heading down the right path.*

ASLEEP AND AWAKE IN GOD

When you go, they [the words of your parents' God]
shall lead you; when you sleep, they shall keep you;
and when you waken, they shall talk with you.
PROVERBS 6:22 AMPC

Some people's parents make it a point to make sure their children are versed in God's power-filled words. Other parents don't, but hopefully a child will end up learning God's wisdom through "spiritual" parents. Either way, knowing God's Word and following it can keep you, Father God's child, from letting your worries careen out of control.

Wherever you go, allow God's Word to lead you down the right path. While you sleep, allow it to comfort and protect you. And when you wake, seek God's Word through reading and His voice through prayer, allowing both to talk to you, giving you all the wisdom you need to keep from stumbling, to make the choices God would have you make throughout your day.

. . . .

Heavenly Father, help me to lean heavily on Your Word.
Talk to me, guide me, comfort and protect me.

THE RIGHT WOMAN FOR THE JOB

Moses said to God, "Who am I that I should
go. . . ?" God answered, "I will be with you."
EXODUS 3:11–12 GW

From a burning bush, God appeared to Moses, telling him to free His people. But Moses was full of worry and self-doubt, so he asked God, "Who am I that I should go?" Then he came up with a bunch of excuses why he wasn't the right man for the job.

Perhaps Moses didn't know that whoever God calls, He's already prepared.

Moses was the only Hebrew who could go in front of the Pharaoh because he'd been an Egyptian prince for forty years. And, having spent another forty years shepherding in the wilderness, Moses was familiar with the terrain. On top of that, God said He'd be with him.

Is God calling you to do something you're not sure you can do? Are you worried you won't be able to handle it? Don't be. Whoever God calls, He's prepared. And just as God was with Moses, He's with you.

. . . .

Lord, I know You've prepared me for
where You call me. Help me trust in You.

WHAT'S IN YOUR HAND?

Moses answered, But behold, they will not believe me or listen to and obey my voice; for they will say, The Lord has not appeared to you. And the Lord said to him, What is that in your hand? And he said, A rod.
EXODUS 4:1–2 AMPC

So God has called you and, like Moses, you still have worries, self-doubts. That's when God calls your attention to the tools you already have, the ones you're very familiar with, the ones in your hand or your company.

For Moses, one tool was his shepherd's staff, which he'd later use to part waters, lead people, strike rocks, turn rivers to blood. Your tool might be your pen, voice, talent, vehicle, knitting needle. Another of Moses' tools was his brother, Aaron, one who could speak well.

Instead of worrying about how you'll do something, look to see what you have in your hand or who you have at your side. Pray for God to reveal your tools, and then use them.

. . . .

What, Lord, would You have me use to serve You? Reveal my tools for Your glory!

DESIRES MET

*Whatever we ask we receive from him,
because we keep his commandments and do what
pleases him. And this is his commandment, that we
believe in the name of his Son Jesus Christ and love
one another, just as he has commanded us.*
1 JOHN 3:22–23 ESV

Worried you won't get what you've been praying for? You needn't be. You *will* get what you desire if you follow God's commands and do what pleases Him.

That means you must believe in Jesus: that He walked upon this earth, was God's Son, performed miracles, was full of wisdom, and is the example you're to follow. The second command is to love others—including God and yourself.

When you're meeting those requirements, when you have the faith God commands, you're living in God's will and so are asking for the things God's hoping you'll ask for and has ready and waiting for you!

Examine your life. Talk to God. Live His way. And your desires will be more than met!

. . . .

*Help me examine my life, Lord. I want
to live—and pray—Your way.*

ALL IS WELL

She said, "All is well."
2 KINGS 4:23 ESV

A childless woman went out of her way to provide a room where Elisha, a man of God, could rest when he came into town. To repay her, Elisha told her she'd have a baby. And she did. A boy. But then he died. So she laid her son on Elisha's bed and went to find Elisha. When her husband asked why she was going out, she simply said, "All is well." She repeated the phrase to Elisha's servant, who, seeing her coming, asked if anything was wrong (see 2 Kings 4:26 ESV). And in the end, all *was* well, for Elisha brought the boy back to life.

Imagine what would've happened if she'd been paralyzed by worry. If she'd kept repeating, "All is wrong." The point? Go the way of this woman. No matter what's happening, know God has a plan. Somehow, He'll make everything turn out right.

. . . .

Lord, I know You make all things work out to Your good. Help me adopt the mantra that no matter what things look like to me, all is well in You.

PRAYING HANDS

*You, O Lord, are a shield for me, my glory, and the
lifter of my head. . . . I lay down and slept; I wakened
again, for the Lord sustains me. I will not be afraid.*
PSALM 3:3, 5–6 AMPC

The world can be a pretty scary place. It's enough to make you wring your hands, leading you to worry about what may be coming around the next corner. But fortunately for you, God is on your side.

Imagine God being a shield that totally surrounds you. That He honors you with His company. That He gives you joy and will deliver you, even in the worst of times, so that you can keep your head above the waters.

Instead of wringing your hands, fold them together and pray. Rest and sleep easy, knowing God sustains you. With Him in your corner, you need not be afraid. His blessing and love are upon you!

. . . .

*You're my shield, Lord. You fill me with joy and keep my
head in the right place. Knowing that You're sustaining
me, I rest and sleep easy. As I pray, my fears fade.*

WATCH AND WAIT

In the morning You hear my voice, O Lord; in the morning I prepare [a prayer, a sacrifice] for You and watch and wait [for You to speak to my heart].
PSALM 5:3 AMPC

One of the best places to have a Bible is right by your bed, for then you can connect with God before your feet even hit the floor. To help you springboard into this idea of making reading the Word a morning habit, begin by reading the psalms, specifically Psalm 5:3.

It acknowledges that God hears your voice in the morning as you prepare a prayer for Him. It reminds you not to just read some words and then jump out of bed, but to pray "and watch and wait" for God to speak to your heart. To give you the exact words that will keep your mind free from worry, give your soul peace, and calm your spirit.

· ·

In the morning You hear my voice, O Lord; in this moment I prepare a prayer for You. And now I watch and wait for You to speak into my heart.

NO WORRY LINES

Let all those who take refuge and put their trust in You rejoice; let them ever sing and shout for joy, because You make a covering over them and defend them; let those also who love Your name be joyful in You and be in high spirits.

PSALM 5:11 AMPC

It's difficult to be joyful in God and in high spirits when worry is clouding not only your day but your judgment. The fact of the matter is that worry not only mars you within but without. You've heard of worry lines, haven't you? Who needs them? Why not replace them with laugh lines?

Today, do just that by running to God. Put your trust in Him alone. You'll soon find yourself breaking out in song and shouting for joy. As you trust in God, leaving all your worries in His hands, He covers you with His love and protection and leads you to triumph. As you live in and laugh with God, your worry lines will soon fade.

. . . .

I'm running to You, God, knowing You're my path to joy!

GOD'S SHIELD OF LOVE

For You, Lord, will bless the [uncompromisingly]
righteous [him who is upright and in right standing
with You]; as with a shield You will surround
him with goodwill (pleasure and favor).
PSALM 5:12 AMPC

When you begin seeking God early, expecting Him to speak to your heart, taking refuge in and trusting Him (see Psalm 5:3, 11), not only will your worries take a backseat to God's presence in your life, but He will bless you in so many other ways! He will show you the way to walk and talk. He'll clear the path before you, be with you just where you are, and watch your back from behind. He will surround you with His shield of love and bless you with His favor!

As your worries fall like scales from your eyes, you will be able to see all God is doing in your life, all the blessings He is putting in your path. Your life will be full of pleasure behind God's shield of abundant love.

. . . .

Lord, surround me with Your shield of love so
that my eyes may see Your blessings in my life.

BLESSED IS THE WOMAN WHO SEEKS WISDOM

"Those who look for me find me. . . . Blessed the woman, who listens to me, awake and ready for me each morning, alert and responsive. . . . When you find me, you find life, real life, to say nothing of GOD's good pleasure."
PROVERBS 8:18, 34–35 MSG

Lady Wisdom was with God before He even formed the earth. She was brought forth before the seas, mountains, and heavens. And she's filled with all the knowledge and understanding you need to keep worries at bay.

But there's a hitch. You need to *look* for her. To *listen* to her. To *seek* her each morning. To be *alert* to her presence and *respond* to her advice. When you do, Wisdom will bless you with more than material wealth, which is fleeting at best. She will bless you with spiritual wealth. You'll be living a life worth living, a true life, as the recipient of God's favor.

Today, replace your worry with God's Wisdom, and begin living for real.

. . . .

Reveal Your truths to me. Give me Your wisdom to replace my worry.

PREVAIL IN PROMISES

*"Don't worry about a thing. Go ahead and do what
you've said. But first make a small biscuit for me
and bring it back here. Then go ahead and make
a meal from what's left for you and your son."*
1 KINGS 17:13 MSG

The prophet Elijah approached a poor widow gathering firewood.
He asked her to bring him water and something to eat. She told
him all she had left was "a handful of flour in a jar and a little oil
in a bottle," just enough to "make a last meal" for herself and her
son (1 Kings 17:12 MSG).

But Elisha told her not to worry, that God promised that her
oil and flour would not run out before God sent rain to end the
drought. Hearing those words, the widow put aside her worries,
waved off her parental instincts, and obeyed Elijah. For the next
two years, God provided as promised.

Have faith. God will provide as promised.

· ·

*Lord, I never want my faith to run dry.
I believe in You and Your promises!*

ARROW PRAYERS

*The king said to me, "What are you requesting?" So I
prayed to the God of heaven. And I said to the king, "If it
pleases the king, and if your servant has found favor in your
sight, that you send me to Judah. . .that I may rebuild it."*
NEHEMIAH 2:4–5 ESV

When Nehemiah, the king of Persia's wine taster, received word
that Jerusalem's wall was broken and her gates burned down,
he wept, then fasted and prayed to God for days. When he
later entered the king's presence, he was still sad. So the king,
seeing his cupbearer's face, asked him what the matter was. This
frightened Nehemiah, for servants were to be cheerful before
their sovereign.

So Nehemiah sent up an arrow prayer—quick and to the
point—to God, knowing he'd get courage and guidance just when
he needed it.

Take your challenges to God as soon as they come. Before
they can turn into worries, shoot up an arrow prayer, knowing
your all-powerful Father is waiting and ready to help.

. . . .

*Lead me to pray to You not just daily but the instant
I need You, Lord. Make me an arrow pray-er!*

BEDTIME PRAYER

*In peace I will both lie down and sleep, for You, Lord,
alone make me dwell in safety and confident trust.*
PSALM 4:8 AMPC

King David, the author of today's psalm, had surely had his share of challenges. As a shepherd boy, he'd had to fight lions and bears to keep his father's sheep safe. Later he'd faced a giant, been chased by King Saul, been betrayed by his son Absalom, and fought countless battles.

You too have lots of challenges. Yet you have a God-Father-King-Shepherd you can run to. One who has rescued, encouraged, provided for, and fought for you time after time. He's answered your prayers, has loved you like no other, has gifted you with eternal life, and has made you, His daughter, a princess. You can count on Him to keep you safe, to watch over you.

So when your head hits the pillow, override your worries with God's Word. Bring today's verse to mind. Repeat it slowly, absorbing its power, and you will find the peace you need for a good night's sleep.

. . . .

*In You, loving Lord, I find the peace to sleep,
for You alone keep me safe and sound.*

WEAVING GOD'S WORD WITHIN

Keep my words; lay up within you my commandments [for use when needed] and treasure them. Keep my commandments and live, and keep my law and teaching as the apple (the pupil) of your eye. Bind them on your fingers; write them on the tablet of your heart.
PROVERBS 7:1–3 AMPC

The more ways you work God's Word into your very being, the less you'll find to worry about. In today's passage, God makes it clear you're to follow His words. To store up His wisdom so you can use it when you need it. To keep your eyes fixed on the teachings of His Son and Spirit. To write God's words on the back of your hand and within your heart.

Today spend time in God's Word. Ask God to reveal the verses He wants you to write on your heart. Meditate on them. Implant them within you. Make them a part of your very being, and you'll find yourself naturally doing as He would have you do.

. . . .

God, engrave Your Word upon my heart.

PRAYING FOR ALL

*I admonish and urge that petitions, prayers, intercessions,
and thanksgivings be offered on behalf of all men. . .
that [outwardly] we may pass a quiet and undisturbed
life [and inwardly] a peaceable one in all godliness
and reverence and seriousness in every way.*
1 TIMOTHY 2:1–2 AMPC

There may be some people in positions of power or authority with whom you disagree or feel uncomfortable. There may be some you think will lead your town, city, state, or country down the wrong road. You worry that they don't have the best interests of you and other people at heart.

Rather than worry about what leaders may or may not do next, the apostle Paul urges you to go to God. To pray for "kings and all who are in positions of authority or high responsibility" (see 1 Timothy 2:2 AMPC). For that's the only way you'll be able to live in peace—within and without.

. . . .

*I want to pray for all people in all positions, Lord.
Help me pray for our leaders so that I can gain
Your blessing of true peace within and without.*

A HEART-TO-HEART ATTITUDE

*When Solomon finished making these prayers
and petitions to the LORD, he stood up in front of
the altar of the LORD, where he had been kneeling
with his hands raised toward heaven.*

1 KINGS 8:54 NLT

Prayer is a form of worship, and everyone has their own prayer posture. Some pray with eyes closed, hands folded, or head bowed. King Solomon kneeled and raised his hands toward heaven.

The point is to not judge how other people pray or worry about what others may say about how *you* pray. As the Reverend Billy Graham said, "It's not the body's posture but the heart's attitude that counts when we pray."

Jesus told the woman at the well, "It's who you are and the way you live that count before God. Your worship must engage your spirit in the pursuit of truth. That's the kind of people the Father is out looking for: those who are simply and honestly themselves before him in their worship" (John 4:23 MSG).

Today, go before God for a heart-to-heart talk, conscious of your own heart attitude. Look for places where you might need to be more of who you truly are as you come before God.

· ·

Here I am, Lord, coming before You, just as I am.

QUALIFIED BY GOD

By ourselves we are not qualified in any way to claim that we can do anything. Rather, God makes us qualified.
2 CORINTHIANS 3:5 GW

The world would have you believe that to be successful, you must have a high degree of self-sufficiency, counting on yourself alone to provide your needs. Yet such an attitude would lead you away from God, your true and loving provider. The God who wants you to live in Him as He lives in you, to be dependent on Him so He can work through you to His glory.

An attitude of self-sufficiency also leads you to worrying about how you'll meet all your needs, and keeps you from praying to the One who provides them.

So the next time worry comes creeping along, look within to see if you're harboring an attitude of self-sufficiency. Ask God to root it out so you can become the woman He created you to be—one dependent on Him alone.

. . . .

Keep me leaning on and relying on You, Lord.
For I know I can do nothing without You.

YOUR BURDEN BEARER,
DAY BY DAY

Blessed be the Lord, Who bears our burdens and carries us day by day, even the God Who is our salvation! Selah [pause, and calmly think of that]!
PSALM 68:19 AMPC

How blessed you are to have a God who loves you so much that He will not only bear your burdens but will carry you! And not just once but every single day! Knowing and truly believing this, living as if it is true (which it is), gives you the peace of mind, heart, body, and spirit you need to live a fabulous life, free of worry! Yet the benefits don't stop there. Along with God bearing your load, He's decided you will be strong (Psalm 68:28, 35)!

Today give God your worries. Believe that He's carrying them— and you. Then enter your day in the strength He gives you.

. . . .

Lord, my worries have been weighing me down. Thank You so much for carrying them—and me—today and every day. Such knowledge gives me the strength I need.

HAPPY AND BLESSED

"Blessed are you among women. . . . Oh, how happy is the woman who believes in God, for he does make his promises to her come true."
LUKE 1:42, 45 PHILLIPS

Gabriel told Mary that God favored her and she would be giving birth to His Son. When she wondered how that would happen, the angel explained the details. Then he told her that her once-barren cousin, Elizabeth, had conceived in her old age. "For no promise of God can fail to be fulfilled" (Luke 1:37 PHILILPS)!

Mary responded, "I belong to the Lord, body and soul. . .let it happen as you say" (Luke 1:38 PHILLIPS). Then she went to visit Elizabeth, who called her blessed, saying, "Happy is the woman who believes in God, for he does make his promises to her come true."

You too can be happy and blessed when you give up your worries and submit yourself to God, who makes the impossible possible and never fails to come through on His promises!

. . . .

I lift my whole self up to You, Lord, knowing You and Your promises come true to those who believe!

BE STILL

God is in the midst of her; she shall not be moved;
God will help her when morning dawns.
PSALM 46:5 ESV

No matter what troubles you're facing or what worries are upon your mind, you have a mighty fortress in God. He's your "refuge and strength, an ever-present help in times of trouble" (Psalm 46:1 GW). Because He is living within you and you're abiding in Him, you cannot be harmed or moved. He brings His full power, all His angels, all His resources, visible and invisible, material and temporal, to aid you. He shields, empowers, and frees you.

God brings His peace to you, telling you, gently, "I've got this. You need not worry." He tells you your role in all this. It's to simply "let be and be still, and know (recognize and understand) that I am God" (Psalm 46:10 AMPC).

Today, make it your aim to let be and be still. Know your God is taking care of everything. He's got this.

. . . .

Oh Lord, help me understand You better. Help
me to be still, to let all things be, to let You
take care of everything—including me.

COME AWAY WITH GOD

His left hand is under my head, and his right hand
embraces me! . . . My beloved speaks and says to me:
"Arise, my love, my beautiful one, and come away."
SONG OF SOLOMON 2:6, 10 ESV

God longs to have an intimate relationship with you. He doesn't want your worries about what may or may not happen to become a barrier between you, to distract you from what He can do and is doing in your life.

To tear down the wall of worry, find a quiet place. Tell God all that's on your mind. Relax as you imagine God right next to you. Say, "[I can feel] his left hand under my head and his right hand embraces me!" (Song of Solomon 2:6 AMPC). Spend as much time as you'd like with Him, enjoying His presence, listening for His voice, hearing what He has to say. Then arise, beautiful one, and go with Him wherever He leads.

. . . .

I can feel Your left hand beneath my head, Your
right hand embracing me. Let me rest in this peace,
surrounded by Your presence and love.

CONTINUAL CARE FROM ABBA

*I will be a Father to you, and you shall be My
sons and daughters, says the Lord Almighty.*
2 CORINTHIANS 6:18 AMPC

When you were little, chances are you ran to your parents when you fell and skinned your knee. They wiped away the blood, cleaned the wound, and bandaged it up. Perhaps they even kissed your boo-boo. Why? Because you were their little one, their precious daughter. They loved you and took care of you.

Now you're a woman, perhaps with children of your own. You may even be taking care of your parents as they once took care of you. And sometimes you find yourself worrying, wondering, *Who'll take care of me when I need help?* The answer is God.

You're God's precious daughter. He tells you, "Even when you're old, I'll take care of you. Even when your hair turns gray, I'll support you. I made you and will continue to care for you. I'll support you and save you" (Isaiah 46:4 GW).

Trust God to help you when you fall—from here to eternity.

. . . .

*Thank You, Daddy God, for always being there for me,
ready to help me when I fall, from now until the end of time.*

THE MASTER PLANNER

*We are God's [own] handiwork. . .recreated in
Christ Jesus. . .that we may do those good works
which God predestined (planned beforehand) for
us [taking paths which He prepared ahead of time],
that we should walk in them [. . .for us to live].*
EPHESIANS 2:10 AMPC

God, the Master Planner, had you in mind before time began,
designed you, then re-created you in Christ so you could be a
part of His grand plan. He has paths He's prepared for you to
take, all so you could live the good life He made ready for you.
But how can you do all God has planned, live the amazing life
He's carved out, if you're saddled by worry?

You're in God's plan, but your worries are not. So stop wringing
your hands. Give God all you can't handle, and settle down in
His peace. Live "the good life which He prearranged and made
ready" for you to live.

* *

*Lord, I'm amazed at the plans You've made for me.
Help me leave my worries behind, settle into Your
peace, and walk down the path You've laid out.*

LAUGHING WITHOUT FEAR

*She is clothed with strength and dignity, and she
laughs without fear of the future. . . . Charm is
deceptive, and beauty does not last; but a woman
who fears the Lord will be greatly praised.*
PROVERBS 31:25, 30 NLT

Proverbs 31:10–31 describes the glowing attributes of God's
ideal woman, giving female followers something to aim for.
She's trustworthy, works hard and willingly, takes care of her
household and family, considers investments, gives to the poor,
and is kind and wise. But the most striking is that "she laughs
without fear of the future"! Perhaps you're wondering, *How can
I get to where she is?*

It's simple. Fear God. Know Him. Worship Him by obeying and
loving Him with all your heart, mind, body, spirit, and soul. This
will give you success in every area of your life! Once you truly
know and obey God, you will realize that you really have nothing
at all to worry about.

. . . .

*I want to know You more, Lord, to follow, obey, and love
You. For then I too may laugh without fear of the future!*

NIGHT WATCHES

*I remember You upon my bed and meditate on
You in the night watches. For You have been my
help, and in the shadow of Your wings will I rejoice.
My whole being follows hard after You and clings
closely to You; Your right hand upholds me.*
PSALM 63:6–8 AMPC

It's late at night, and you should be fast asleep. But for some reason, you're still awake. In the quiet darkness, it's easy to let your mind wander into the even darker territory of worry. But why not switch up your thought pattern and go from worry to wonder by meditating on God?

Remember how much God has done for you. How He protected and cared for you, helped you, and provided all you needed to make it to this point in your day and in your life. Rejoice in and thank Him for all the blessings He has bestowed upon you. Then see yourself clinging to Him as He holds you up, carries you, and pours out upon you His strength and peace.

. . . .

*Hold me, Lord, as I cling to You,
absorbing Your presence and peace.*

LET PEACE REIGN

*I have told you these things, so that in Me you may
have [perfect] peace and confidence. In the world you
have tribulation and trials and distress and frustration;
but be of good cheer [take courage; be confident,
certain, undaunted]! For I have overcome the world.*
JOHN 16:33 AMPC

Jesus knows you'll have times of trouble. Yet as you live in Him,
you'll find that perfect peace and confidence you need to face
them. So no matter what has happened, is happening, or may
happen, don't worry.

Instead, take courage. Live the life God has planned for you.
Have confidence in Jesus and have peace within because He
has overcome your world. He says, "I have deprived it of power
to harm you and have conquered it for you" (John 16:33 AMPC).

As you go about your tasks today, give Jesus full access to
your heart, mind, body, spirit, and soul. Allow His peace to reign
over you. In Him, you will become an overcomer.

. . . .

*Come live in me, Jesus. Help me overcome
my worry, and let Your peace reign within.*

IN STEP WITH GOD

*It is the Lord Who goes before you; He will [march]
with you; He will not fail you or let you go or
forsake you; [let there be no cowardice or flinching,
but] fear not, neither become broken [in spirit—
depressed, dismayed, and unnerved with alarm].*
DEUTERONOMY 31:8 AMPC

Moses was saying farewell to God's people, who would be led
into the Promised Land by Joshua. He told them God *Himself*
would go before them and give them victory. He encouraged
them by saying, "Be strong, courageous, and firm; fear not nor
be in terror before them, for it is the Lord your God Who goes
with you" (Deuteronomy 31:6 AMPC).

As God went before His Israelites, He goes before you. He
marches with you as you enter His land of promises. Your role
is to not worry or fear but to believe God will neither fail nor
forsake you. When you trust God with all, keeping in step with
Him, you will prevail.

. . . .

*I'm trusting in You, Lord, as we walk in step
together. Lead me to the land of Your promise.*

CROSSING SAFELY

*I, the LORD your God, hold your right hand; it is I who
say to you, "Fear not, I am the one who helps you."*
ISAIAH 41:13 ESV

A mom becomes extra vigilant when it comes to helping her child cross the street. It is she and not the child who can see all the cars coming, understands the rules of the road, and knows the dangers of stepping away from the safety of the sidewalk. Yet the child is neither fearful nor worried. She's totally secure with her hand in her mom's, knowing with a certainty that this woman will keep her safe from all dangers, seen and unseen, known and unknown.

Now that you're older, you may not need help crossing the street. But you *do* need help finding your way through life. Fortunately, you have Father God beside you. He sees all the dangers that lie ahead. Allow Him to take your right hand. Hear Him say, "Fear not, I am the one who helps you." And you'll find the safety and security you seek.

· ·

Lord, take my hand. Walking with You, I have no fear.

GOD HAS A PLAN

*"I know what I'm doing. I have it all planned out—
plans to take care of you, not abandon you, plans to
give you the future you hope for. When you call on
me, when you come and pray to me, I'll listen."*
JEREMIAH 29:11–12 MSG

Have you ever tried a new recipe and gotten flustered because you didn't know what you were doing? You're worried it won't end up looking just like the picture or tasting like it should?

Some new challenges in life can be like that. No matter how much you plan or how much effort you put into some new task, job, or project, you worry things will somehow go wrong and you may not be able to fix them!

Fortunately, God knows what *He's* doing—and He's infallible, so you need not worry about anything. God has everything planned out for you. He's going to take care of you, "to give you the future you hope for." So no worries. Just go to God in prayer. He's ready to listen.

· ·

*I'm thankful that You know what You're
doing, Lord. I'm counting on You!*

GOING AFTER GOD

You will seek Me, inquire for, and require Me [as a vital necessity] and find Me when you search for Me with all your heart. I will be found by you, says the Lord, and I will release you from captivity.
JEREMIAH 29:13–14 AMPC

When you *really* go looking for God, seeking His face, pining for His presence, needing Him as you need no one and nothing else, searching for Him with all your heart, you will find Him. And when you find Him, God will free you from everything that binds you, including worry.

Can you imagine living a worry-free life? Living every day for God with courage, hope, joy, and laughter? No longer regretting what happened in the past, worrying about what's going on in the present, or fearing the future?

Go after God with all that you are and have. Live a life of freedom. You'll never look back!

. . . .

I'm making You number one in my life, Lord, going after You with all I am and have! Let's do this!

THE ART OF LIFE

The steps of a [good] man are directed and established by the Lord when He delights in his way [and He busies Himself with his every step]. Though he falls, he shall not be utterly cast down, for the Lord grasps his hand in support and upholds him.
PSALM 37:23–24 AMPC

Can you imagine exchanging worry for wonder? It's possible. Journalist Malcom Muggeridge wrote, "Every happening, great and small, is a parable whereby God speaks to us, and the art of life is to get the message."

Instead of focusing on what may or may not happen or how to fix the past, why not wonder what God may be saying to you in the present? Come out of yourself and into God, looking for His message through His Word, for the connection among you, Him, and your life events. See where God's directing you, where He's taking you.

Delight with wonder in every step along the way, knowing that with your hand in Father God's, although you may stumble, He'll never let you fall.

. . . .

*Lord, help me discover Your message as
I delight in every step along the way.*

NO WORD WITHOUT POWER

For with God nothing is ever impossible and no word from God shall be without power or impossible of fulfillment.

Luke 1:37 AMPC

You found yourself in a situation where you don't know what to do or say. You have a problem that seems unsolvable. You have a challenge before you that seems overwhelming. Fears and worries begin preying on your mind. How will you ever find your way out of this one?

When you're between a rock and a hard place and see no way out, look to God. Rest in His presence. Bask in His peace. Remind yourself that there's no feat He cannot perform, no task He cannot undertake, no problem He cannot solve, no challenge He cannot meet. Nothing is impossible for God. He makes all His words and promises come true. And He's your number one fan.

· ·

I don't know what to do, Lord. That's where You come in. Help! I'm trusting in You to make things right. Ease me with the power of Your Word!

PERFECT LOVE

And as we live in God, our love grows more perfect.
So we will not be afraid. . . . Such love has no fear.
1 JOHN 4:17–18 NLT

As you purpose to live in God's love, you're not only living in Him, but He's living in you! Communing with Him, there's no room for anything else—no worries, no fears, no anger, no doubts. God loves you so much that He'll never let anything come between you and Him. Nor will He let anything or anyone snatch you out of His hand (John 10:28–30).

Today, pray that God will help you open your heart to the power and peace of His love, that your spirit and His will meld into one. Then spend some time in God's presence, allowing His love to pour into you, feed and nourish you, and fill you until it spills out of you and onto those around you.

. . . .

Lord, I want that perfect love I get only when I am living in Your love and You're living in me. Fill me, Lord, with such love.

ONE THING WORTH YOUR ATTENTION

The Lord said to her, "My dear Martha, you are worried and upset over all these details! There is only one thing worth being concerned about. Mary has discovered it, and it will not be taken away from her."
LUKE 10:41–42 NLT

Are you a Martha or a Mary?

Martha had invited Jesus to come into her house. But while she was rushing around preparing food for Jesus and the other guests, her sister, Mary, "sat at the Lord's feet, listening to what he taught" (Luke 10:39 NLT). So Martha went to Jesus, saying, "Lord, doesn't it seem unfair to you that my sister just sits here while I do all the work? Tell her to come and help me" (Luke 10:40 NLT). That's when Jesus made it clear that Martha shouldn't be worried or upset. There was only one thing to focus on—Jesus and His words.

Today, turn your worries over to Jesus. Let Him know you're interested in one thing only—listening to what He has to say.

. . . .

Here I am, Lord, sitting at Your feet.
Please speak to me. I'm listening.

BECOMING UNSINKABLE

*Jesus immediately reached out his hand
and took hold of him, saying to him, "O you
of little faith, why did you doubt?"*
MATTHEW 14:31 ESV

After telling His followers to take the boat to the other side of the lake, Jesus went up on a mountain to pray. When darkness set in, the boat was still far from the shore, caught in a storm.

So Jesus came to them, walking on the water. When the disciples saw Him, they cried out in fear. But Jesus immediately told them, "Take heart; it is I. Do not be afraid" (Matthew 14:27 ESV). That's when Peter got brave, saying, "If it's You, Jesus, tell me to come to You." Jesus did, prompting Peter to get out of the boat and begin walking on the water. But then he saw the wind, got scared, and began sinking, crying out to Jesus, "Save me!" And Jesus did!

The point? If you keep your eyes on Jesus, focusing on Him rather than your circumstances, Jesus will enable you to do things you never dreamed possible!

. . . .

With You, Jesus, I'm unsinkable! Tell me to come to You!

SPEAK EASY

"Don't worry in advance about what to say. Just say what God tells you at that time, for it is not you who will be speaking, but the Holy Spirit."
MARK 13:11 NLT

How many times have you had a difficult life scene to play out? So you rehearsed in your mind exactly what you'd say, sometimes even imagining what the other person's response would be.

There are a couple of problems with that method. The first is that the conversation that actually ends up taking place is rarely the same as what you imagined. The second is that by worrying in advance about what you're going to say and then trying to stick to that script leaves no room for the Holy Spirit to get a word in edgewise!

The best way to handle what may be a difficult conversation is to go to God. Let Him know what's going on, what you're concerned about. Then relax. "Just say what God tells you," for it won't be you who's speaking but the Spirit.

. . . .

*Spirit, when I don't know what to say,
speak through me, I pray.*

CHOOSE JOY

*"He shall eat curds and honey when he knows
how to refuse the evil and choose the good."*
Isaiah 7:15 ESV

Every day you have the freedom to make choices. To choose good over evil, right over wrong, God's Way over your way, and joy over worry. That's a lot of choices, each one having its own set of repercussions. The choosing good over evil, right over wrong, and God's Way over your own seems self-explanatory. You ask God what to do and you do it.

But how do you choose joy over worry? It's simple: You open your eyes to the blessings around you.

Author Marianne Williamson wrote, "Joy is what happens when we allow ourselves to recognize how good things really are." Today—and every day—choose to do just that. Write a list of things that are going right in your life. Then thank God for all He has done for you, and your joy will blossom.

. . . .

*Help me, Lord, to choose joy, to recognize all the
good in my life, in other people, and in this world.*

BREATHING IN PEACE

"Peace be with you! As the Father has sent me, so I am sending you." After he had said this, he breathed on the disciples and said, "Receive the Holy Spirit."
JOHN 20:21–22 GW

The disciples gathered together behind locked doors, worried what the Jews might do. It was there the resurrected Jesus appeared, saying, "Peace be with you!" He showed them His wounds, and then repeated His greeting of peace, adding that He was sending them out. Then He breathed on them, saying, "Receive the Holy Spirit."

As a believer, you've been gifted with the Holy Spirit. Yet to do what you have been called to do, to be fully focused on the work and not the worry, you're to open yourself up to the peace and breath of Christ through prayer.

Edwin Keith wrote that "prayer is exhaling the spirit of man and inhaling the spirit of God." Today, imagine that's just what you're doing as you pray.

. . . .

Lord Jesus, bring me Your peace as I pray, exhaling the spirit of woman and inhaling the Spirit of God.

RADIANT WITH HOPE

*May the God of hope fill you with joy and peace in
your faith, that by the power of the Holy Spirit, your
whole life and outlook may be radiant with hope.*
ROMANS 15:13 PHILLIPS

Tired of letting your worries fill your mind, guide your decisions, and keep you from living the life God wants you to live? Why not fill your mind with God before worry has a chance to rear its ugly head?

Artist Howard Chandler Christy had a good method you might want to follow. He said, "Every morning I spend fifteen minutes filling my mind full of God; and so there's no room left for worry thoughts." Sounds like a plan!

This morning, before your mind has a chance to run away with itself, fill it full of God. Begin with a short, "Good morning, Glory!" prayer. Then read a portion of the Bible, looking for a message from the Author of your faith. Finally, pray as the Spirit leads, allowing Him to give you His outlook, radiant with hope!

· ·

Good morning, Glory! Fill my mind, give me hope!

THE TRUE YOU

*"That's why my cup is running over. This is
the assigned moment for him to move into the
center, while I slip off to the sidelines."*
JOHN 3:29–30 MSG

The Bible tells you to offer yourself up to God, to allow Jesus to become more while you become less. Yet you may wonder where that will leave you, your personality, your uniqueness.

There's no need to worry. As C. S. Lewis wrote in *Mere Christianity*:

The more we get what we now call "ourselves" out of the way and let Him take us over, the more truly ourselves we become. . . . It is when I turn to Christ, when I give myself up to His Personality, that I first begin to have a real personality of my own.*

Today, let Jesus take you over so that you can become the true you everyone (including God) is waiting to meet.

. . . .

*Jesus, forgive me for holding back, for not giving
all of myself over to You. Help me get out of the
way so that You and I can truly shine!*

EVERY MOMENT BECOMES A PRAYER

Seek GOD while he's here to be found,
pray to him while he's close at hand.
ISAIAH 55:6 MSG

God wants you to seek Him, to pray to Him while He's near. But as you're striving to meet project deadlines, get your chores done, pick up the kids, volunteer at church, and so much more, prayer seems to fall by the wayside. You begin worrying God sees you as a slacker. How can you pray without ceasing when you barely have time to fit in a shower?

God didn't devise prayer to be just one more to-do. So perhaps it's time to change your perspective of prayer.

Frank Bianco, a journalist and photographer, wrote, "If you begin to live life looking for the God that is all around you, every moment becomes a prayer." Try doing that today, seeing God in everything that surrounds you and lifting up your thanks as you live in God's wonderland.

. . . .

Reveal Yourself to me, Lord, in all I do and see.
Make every moment of my life a prayer to You.

SOUL HARMONY

Let the peace (soul harmony which comes) from Christ rule (act as umpire continually) in your hearts [deciding and settling with finality all questions that arise in your minds, in that peaceful state].
COLOSSIANS 3:15 AMPC

Does the peace of Christ rule over your heart? Or does worry have full sway? Perhaps it's a toss-up, depending on what's going on in your life.

It's easy to have a calm demeanor if everything's going just the way you want it to. The challenge comes when God pulls you out of your comfort zone or things beyond your control begin going haywire.

Yet if you trust God no matter what's happening in your life, you'll not only have peace within but be radiating it without. And that's what will make you a great witness for your faith. As William J. Toms wrote, "Be careful how you live. You may be the only Bible some person ever reads."

Make it your aim to let Christ's peace reign. You'll be amazed how His Light within you will attract others without.

. . . .

*Lord, may Your peace rule over my heart,
calming me within and attracting others without.*

A GOOD MEASURE

"Give, and it will be given to you. Good measure,
pressed down, shaken together, running over,
will be put into your lap. For with the measure
you use it will be measured back to you."
LUKE 6:38 ESV

Jesus wants you to treat others well, for when you bless them, God will bless you back. Yet it may be difficult to give of yourself or your resources when you're worried you won't "have enough" for yourself.

It's time to change up that mindset. Let your worries of lack fall by the wayside, and start making this world a better place by giving to others, whether by serving in church, volunteering at a food bank, donating to a charity, helping a neighbor plant a garden, or giving a blanket to a homeless shelter.

Begin by doing one little thing for someone you know or even a complete stranger. Write down what you've done, including how you were rewarded in return, and soon your worries around lack will be a dim memory.

* *

Show me what I can do today,
Jesus, to bless the life of another.

ALL YOU NEED

I give thanks to Him Who has granted me [the needed] strength and made me able [for this], Christ Jesus our Lord, because He has judged and counted me faithful and trustworthy, appointing me to [this stewardship of] the ministry.
1 TIMOTHY 1:12 AMPC

You've been offered to help out with a ministry, to perhaps even be in charge of it, but you're worried you may not have the time or energy to take it on. Or you're already serving somewhere and worried you might be running out of steam. This is where prayer is more important than ever.

God has definite plans for you. And Jesus is the One who gives you the strength to do what you're called to do. So before you say yes to anything new or remain where you are, go to Him in prayer. Ask if this is where He wants you to begin or continue. Then serve Him well, confident that He'll give you all the supernatural power and ability you need—and more.

. . . .

Lord, thank You for giving me the direction, power, and ability I need to serve You well!

BEAMING WITH LOVE

*Neither death nor life, neither messenger of Heaven
nor monarch of earth, neither what happens today
nor what may happen tomorrow, neither a power from
on high nor a power from below, nor anything else
in God's whole world has any power to separate us
from the love of God in Jesus Christ our Lord!*
ROMANS 8:38–39 PHILLIPS

People may come against you. They may even walk out of your life or stop loving you. But you need not worry that you will ever be separated from God's love, for His love is unconditional. No matter what happens, He will love you. His love is an unbreakable cord between you and Him.

Pray that God will open your heart to His love. That you will feel that joyful love beaming down into you, surrounding you, cushioning you, holding you, blessing you, warming you, feeding you every moment of this day, giving you the confidence to walk His way regardless of what others do and say.

. . . .

Abba God, beam Your love into my heart as I rest in You.

153

A PLACE FOR YOU

*"You must not let yourselves be distressed—you must
hold on to your faith in God and to your faith in me.
There are many rooms in my Father's House. . . .
I am going away to prepare a place for you. . . . I am
coming again to welcome you into my own home."*
JOHN 14:1–3 PHILLIPS

Jesus doesn't want you to worry about anything. Instead, He tells you to hold on to your faith in God and in Him! Even though He has physically left this earth, He's left you a Helper (the Holy Spirit). Meanwhile He, Jesus, has gone ahead to get your room ready—in His house, no less! Why? So you can be where He is (John 14:4)!

So set your worries aside. Hold on to your faith in Jesus and Father God. Live without a care as you follow the Way, the Truth, and the Life in Him, looking forward to the room awaiting you in His home sweet home.

. . . .

*You, Jesus, are already my home away from home.
Thank You for preparing a place just for me—with You!*

THE WOMAN WHO STICKS WITH GOD

"Blessed is the man who trusts me, GOD, the woman who sticks with GOD. They're like trees. . .putting down roots near the rivers—never a worry through the hottest of summers, never dropping a leaf, serene and calm through droughts."
JEREMIAH 17:7–8 MSG

Not only does worry sap your strength and energy, it also keeps you from creating, from being productive. God knows this only too well. That's why He tells you that you're blessed when you trust in Him and stick with Him and His plan. When you believe His promises.

When you trust in God, He says you're like a tree with roots that have access to His river of life. Even through the hottest drought, you'll still be fresh. By being confident in Him, calm and serene, you'll be "bearing fresh fruit every season" (Jeremiah 17:8 MSG).

Trust God. And you'll be blessed in all things, at all times, and in all ways.

. . . .

I'm sticking with You, Lord, refusing to let winds of worry have any sway over me.

STANDING FIRM

"Say to him, 'Be careful, be quiet, do not fear, and do not let your heart be faint. . . . Because Syria, with Ephraim and the son of Remaliah, has devised evil against you. . . . Thus says the Lord GOD: It shall not stand, and it shall not come to pass.'"
ISAIAH 7:4–5, 7 ESV

Some countries had threatened Judah. So God told Isaiah to tell King Ahaz "to stop worrying. Tell him he doesn't need to fear" (Isaiah 7:4 NLT). Even though others had planned evil against him, it would never take place, it wouldn't come to pass.

When worries come ready to attack you, listen to what God says. "Stop worrying. You don't need to fear." Besides, most of what you worry about will never happen! And even if it does, God will work it out for good.

So have faith in God. Trust in Him. "If you don't take your stand in faith, you won't have a leg to stand on" (Isaiah 7:9 MSG).

. . . .

*I'm standing firm in my faith, Lord,
trusting in You—no matter what comes!*

YOUR BEST DEFENSE

"Don't be afraid! Stand still, and see what the LORD will do to save you today. You will never see these Egyptians again. The LORD is fighting for you! So be still!"
EXODUS 14:13–14 GW

God had taken His people out of their comfort zone, and their worry grew to panic. They began thinking it would be better if they were slaves back in Egypt instead of between the Egyptian army and the Red Sea. But Moses told them not to worry or be afraid, to merely stand still and watch what God was going to do. They'd never see these warriors again because God was fighting for them.

And God won the day! He parted the sea for His people and brought the waters back to drown the attackers.

You're God's daughter, one of His people. He'll defend you no matter what. Your job is not to worry or panic but to stand still and watch Him work!

. . . .

You, Lord, are my best and most powerful defense. As for me, I'm going to simply stand still and watch You win the day!

THE ROAD MAP
TO A CAREFREE LIFE

Godliness with contentment is great gain, for we brought nothing into the world, and we cannot take anything out of the world. But if we have food and clothing, with these we will be content.
1 TIMOTHY 6:6–8 ESV

What's on your worry list? Are you fretting that you won't have enough money to buy that new purse you've been wanting? Are you worrying you won't be able to keep making payments on that new car? Perhaps it's time to make some life adjustments.

The apostle Paul says that being right with God and happy with what you have is what really satisfies. As long as you have food in your belly and clothing on your being, you should and can be content.

So don't worry about getting more stuff if it's going to put you into debt or keep you chained to something you don't really need. Instead, look to please God and follow Jesus. That's the road map to a carefree life!

. . . .

Help me live more simply, Lord, so I can live with less worry—and less stuff!

TRUST IN THE LORD

Don't worry about the wicked or envy those who do
wrong. For like grass, they soon fade away. Like spring
flowers, they soon wither. Trust in the LORD and do good.
Then you will live safely in the land and prosper.
PSALM 37:1–3 NLT

Sometimes it seems those who get all the breaks are the people who don't believe in God. In fact, the more they lie and cheat, going against all rules and laws, the more they seem to prosper! Yet here you are, doing the right thing, at least most of the time, and you can't seem to get ahead.

God tells you not to worry about those who are walking down the dark path. It's *you* who's truly prospering. While you're on the road to eternal life, storing up treasures in heaven, the ne'er-do-wells will quickly fade away, unable to take their gains with them.

So take heart. Trust in God, leaving everything and everyone in His hands. He'll make things come out right.

Lord, help me keep my eyes on You and what
You'd have me do—for in You I truly prosper!

DELIGHT IN GOD

Delight yourself also in the Lord, and He will give you the desires and secret petitions of your heart.
PSALM 37:4 AMPC

You've had a secret desire for ages, a dream that you've wanted to pursue since you were a child, but the timing has never seemed to be right. Now you're worried, wondering if you'll ever get to realize your dream. Perhaps it's too late!

Rest easy. As long as you keep coming to God, spending time with Him, delighting in His presence and Word, "He will give you the desires and secret petitions of your heart." With God, it's never too late.

Today, pray to God. Tell Him your desires. Ask Him what He would have you do. He'll be sure to put you on the right path to bring glory to Him and joy to you.

. . . .

Here I am, Lord, delighting in Your Word, finding joy and peace in Your presence. Let's talk about dreams and desires. Where would You have me go? What would You have me do?

COMMIT YOUR WAY TO GOD

Commit your way to the Lord [roll and repose each care of your load on Him]; trust (lean on, rely on, and be confident) also in Him and He will bring it to pass. And He will make your uprightness and right standing with God go forth as the light.
PSALM 37:5–6 AMPC

Wondering about where to go, what to do? Worried you might have taken a wrong turn somewhere? Relax. Let God know all of your concerns. Allow them to roll off your back and onto His. Trust that the Master Planner will show you the way you're to go.

God hasn't left you alone. He, His Son Jesus, and the Holy Spirit are here to watch over and look out for you. They know the past, present, and future, hold all wisdom, and wield supernatural power. They see what you're doing, where you're going, what you're thinking, and where your heart is. Open yourself to them, be responsive to their prompts, and you will never lose your way.

· ·

Show me the way, Lord, as I shine for You!

BE PATIENT

*Be still and rest in the Lord; wait for Him and patiently
lean yourself upon Him; fret not yourself.*
PSALM 37:7 AMPC

It's all in the timing, you think, as you chew your fingernails down
to the quick. *But when will God act? How long do I need to wait?
Maybe I should be doing something to help speed things along
. . .but what?*

Have you ever had these thoughts while you anxiously waited
for God to do something—or just anything? If so, you may have
been getting dangerously close to doing something out of God's
will for you, which rarely, if ever, turns out well. Just ask Sarah
and Rebecca (see Genesis 16 and 27).

Rather than worry about when God will move, just be still and
rest in His presence. Wait patiently for Him to act. He has the
perfect timing.

. . . .

*Help me, Lord, to be still and at peace and to
wait for You to move before I step out of line.
I know You have the perfect timing.*

BY GOD'S POWER

*"They will pass safely through the sea of distress, for the waves of the sea will be held back, and the waters. . .will dry up. . . . By my power I will make my people strong, and by my authority they will go wherever they wish. I, the L*ORD*, have spoken!"*
ZECHARIAH 10:11–12 NLT

When you feel as if you're drowning in troubles, don't worry or lose heart. Instead, pray. Ask God to remind you He's more powerful than any other being and that He'll make sure you get safely through that sea of distress. He'll hold back the waves that threaten your life and dry up the deepest parts of the water. Your Father can do all that because He's God! Because when He speaks, things happen!

God will not only save you but strengthen you and lead you where you want to go. Listen: God has spoken! Believe: And you will conquer!

. . . .

Thank You, Lord, for being with me in the depths and heights of this life. Hold back the waves when they threaten to overwhelm. Keep me strong in You!

GOOD TALKS

Let no corrupting talk come out of your mouths,
but only such as is good for building up, as fits the
occasion, that it may give grace to those who hear.
EPHESIANS 4:29 ESV

Your words have power, affecting those around you. That's why you must be careful not to pollute another person's thoughts with your worries. By voicing them, you may cause others to take on your worries as their own while reinforcing your concerns in your own mind. Before you know it, your proposed what-ifs have become contagious, full-blown fears!

Instead of voicing worries, consider saying uplifting things to yourself and others, such as, "We can do all things with Christ's strength" (see Philippians 4:13). Or, "God will make a way." Or, "I believe I'll see the goodness of the Lord in this world" (see Psalm 27:13). Whatever fits the occasion.

In saying good things, you'll be building up the faith of others as well as your own!

. . . .

Lord, help me speak words of Your wisdom instead of
voicing my worries. Make me a builder not a wrecker.

WAITING ON GOD

Those who wait for the Lord [who expect, look for, and hope in Him] shall change and renew their strength and power; they shall lift their wings and mount up [close to God] as eagles [mount up to the sun]; they shall run and not be weary, they shall walk and not faint or become tired.
Isaiah 40:31 AMPC

Worry can be so draining on the mind, body, spirit, and soul. When you're walking through this life exhausted, you'll more easily stumble somewhere along the way.

Rather than worry, wait on God. Expect Him to work in your life. Look for Him everywhere, smiling when you see evidence of His love, power, and compassion. Put all your hope in Him alone.

When you do, you'll find yourself refreshed, able to take on whatever comes your way. You'll be renewed in strength and power, mounting up higher and ever closer to the Son. You'll run and not get tired. You'll walk and not faint.

Wait in and on God. He'll keep you strong.

. . . .

I'm waiting, Lord, lifting myself up to You in heavenly flight.

A FAITH-FILLED WOMAN

I am calling up memories of your sincere and unqualified faith (the leaning of your entire personality on God in Christ in absolute trust and confidence in His power, wisdom, and goodness), [a faith] that first lived permanently in [the heart of] your grandmother Lois and your mother Eunice and now, I am [fully] persuaded, [dwells] in you also.
2 Timothy 1:5 AMPC

How you live out your faith makes an impression on young minds. When your children and grandchildren or someone else's children look at your life, will they see you as a female fretter or a woman warrior?

The apostle Paul was Timothy's spiritual father. In his letter to the young man, Paul recalls Timothy's mother and grandmother, how their sincere faith was an example for Timothy to follow, paving the way for him to totally believe in Christ.

May you, like Timothy's mother and grandmother, become much more of a prayer warrior than a worrier, a peace- and faith-filled woman whom others can look to and emulate.

* *

*Dear Lord, make me a prayerful woman,
full of peace and strong in faith.*

LIVING GOD'S TRUTH

*"Do not be afraid, for I have ransomed you. I have called
you by name; you are mine. When you go through deep
waters, I will be with you. When you go through rivers
of difficulty, you will not drown. When you walk through
the fire of oppression, you will not be burned up."*
ISAIAH 43:1–2 NLT

When you're going through tough times, you needn't give in to worry because God is with you. As you go through a torrent of troubles, you won't drown. And when you walk through the flames of cruelty, you won't get burned.

You'll be saved because you're God's precious daughter! He honors and loves you! Even if you wander off, God says, "I will say to the north, 'Give them up,' and to the south, 'Do not keep them.' Bring. . .my daughters from the ends of the earth" (Isaiah 43:6 GW).

When worries start piling up, remember who you are in God's eyes, and pray to the Father who loves you, the One who calls you by name.

. . . .

*I want to live Your truth, Father God.
Walk with me as I grow in You.*

SOMETHING NEW

The LORD makes a path through the sea and a road through the strong currents. . . . Forget what happened in the past, and do not dwell on events from long ago. I am going to do something new. It is already happening. Don't you recognize it?
ISAIAH 43:16, 18–19 GW

God is the only being powerful enough to actually make a path through the sea, a road through the riptide. But you'll never see that new path or road if you're spending your time today ruminating over what happened yesterday.

God wants you living in the present moment, expecting the unexpected. He's going to do something totally new in your life. In fact, He's already doing it! Do you see it? He's going to "clear a way in the desert," to "make rivers on dry land" (Isaiah 43:19 GW).

So put your worries about the past behind you. Keep your eyes open to where God's working! You'll be sure to see a new path ahead.

. . . .

Lord, I'm ready to expect the unexpected! My eyes are focused on the new road You've already paved ahead!

TAKE HEED

Take heed to yourselves and be on your guard,
lest your hearts be overburdened and depressed
(weighed down) with the. . .worldly worries and
cares pertaining to [the business of] this life.
LUKE 21:34 AMPC

First one little worry creeps into your mind. Sometime later a what-if joins the first one. Then another, and another, and another come. Soon you can barely breathe. You can't lift yourself up. You have no strength to clear out your mind, heart, spirit, and soul of all the worries weighing you down.

Jesus wants you to stay on your guard and to be alert to when the cares of this world come creeping in. When the first fret tries to gain access to you, go to God. Ask Him to relieve you, to give you a Bible verse to ward off that particular worry. As you make this a habit, you'll find yourself filled with the blessings of God's wisdom and truth rather than the curses of the evil one's worries and lies.

. . . .

Help me be more vigilant, Lord, and replace
my worries with Your wisdom.

THE SPIRIT OF FREEDOM

*Those who trust God's action in them find that God's
Spirit is in them—living and breathing God! Obsession
with self in these matters is a dead end; attention to God
leads us out into the open, into a spacious, free life.*
ROMANS 8:6–7 MSG

Worry is a reminder that every moment you have a choice as to what kind of life you want to live—in the spirit or in the flesh. If your mind is on the flesh, you become an enslaved worrier, but if your mind is on God's Spirit, you become God's free warrior.

It comes down to where your focus is. The Message puts it this way: "Focusing on the self is the opposite of focusing on God. Anyone completely absorbed in self ignores God, ends up thinking more about self than God. That person ignores who God is and what he is doing" (Romans 8:8).

Today choose to trust in God and be a free woman warrior.

. . . .

*Lord, lead me out of myself and into You,
where I'll find the peace and freedom I crave.*

SING ALONG

The Lord your God is in the midst of you, a Mighty One, a Savior [Who saves]! He will rejoice over you with joy; He will rest [in silent satisfaction] and in His love He will be silent and make no mention [of past sins, or even recall them].
ZEPHANIAH 3:17 AMPC

When you're writing an email, it's easy enough to fix and forget your mistakes by hitting the DELETE button. If you're using a pencil to work out a math problem, an eraser rectifies any errors. But you may find it more difficult to fix and forget the mistakes you make in what you say or do in your life.

Yet God wants you to know that when you've misstepped and asked Him for forgiveness, He not only doesn't bring up your errors but forgets all about them! And He "exult[s] over you with singing" (Zephaniah 3:17 AMPC)!

So don't worry about your past mistakes. Forget about them, just like God has. Then join in the singing!

. . . .

Thank You for always forgiving me when I mess up, Lord. Lead me in song with You!

GOD QUIETS POUNDING WAVES

You faithfully answer our prayers with awesome deeds,
O God our savior. You are the hope of everyone on
earth. . . . You formed the mountains by your power
and armed yourself with mighty strength. You quieted
the raging oceans with their pounding waves.
PSALM 65:5–7 NLT

You may have some worries that are deeply rooted. They're old and full of power, keeping you from easily being freed of them. That's when you need to reach out more than once (perhaps multiple times) and call on God, the Master of awesome deeds.

God has not only formed all that you see around you—including you—but all that lies beyond you in this world and the next. He is a supernatural being with more power than you can even begin to imagine. Trust Him to quiet those waves of worries deep within you. To stop them from pounding upon your inner spirit. To extinguish them altogether.

Pray, and God will faithfully answer with awesome deeds.

. . . .

Lord, free me of the power of this worry. . .
My hope lies in You alone.

BUILDING HOPE

Oh! May the God of green hope fill you up with joy, fill you up with peace, so that your believing lives, filled with the life-giving energy of the Holy Spirit, will brim over with hope!
ROMANS 15:13 MSG

Dictionary.com defines *hope* as "the feeling that what is wanted can be had or that events will turn out for the best" or "grounds for this feeling in a particular instance." That's an awesome quality to acquire, for it seems hope would naturally ward off worry!

Make it your aim to build up your hope in God. Scour the Bible for verses about hope. Memorize them, perhaps beginning with today's verse. Or maybe Psalm 42:5 (ESV): "Why are you cast down, O my soul, and why are you in turmoil within me? Hope in God; for I shall again praise him."

Remember, you are the daughter of the King, the Master, the Creator who has "plans to give you a future filled with hope" (Jeremiah 29:11 GW).

. . . .

*God of hope, fill me up with Your joy and peace
so that I'll be brimming over with hope!*

OUT OF THE PIT

"I called out your name, O GOD, called from the bottom of the pit. You listened when I called out, 'Don't shut your ears! Get me out of here! Save me!' You came close when I called out. You said, 'It's going to be all right.'"
LAMENTATIONS 3:56–57 MSG

When your worries have you feeling as if you're at the bottom of a dark pit, your avenue back into the light is to call out from the depths. Call God by one of the many names that describe His character and fit your need—God Almighty, Defender, Strong Tower, the God Who Watches Over Me, Refuge, Shield, the Lord My Rock, Lord of Light.

Know that God *will* hear you and listen to what you say. He *will* get you out of the depths of darkness and into His Light. As He sidles up next to you, you'll hear His reassuring words, "It's going to be all right."

. . . .

Lord of Light and Life, free me from this pit of worry! Come close when I call!

GOD PLANS GOOD

"Even though you planned evil against me,
God planned good to come out of it. This was
to keep many people alive, as he is doing now."
GENESIS 50:20 GW

Joseph was the favored son of his father, Jacob. One day, out of jealousy, Joseph's brothers threw him into a pit then sold him to traders. He was bought by an officer of Pharaoh of Egypt, unjustly accused of rape, and thrown into a dungeon. Yet through all these things, Joseph never worried but trusted in God. No matter what happened or where he landed, "The LORD was with Joseph, so he became a successful man" (Genesis 39:2 GW). Eventually Joseph was made the number two man in Egypt. As such, he was able to save his family.

Even though you may be going through some tough times, don't worry. Trust that God has a purpose for you. No matter what happens, have faith that God is planning good to come out of it. And you too will be successful.

. . . .

Thank You, Lord, for loving me. I'm trusting in Your
purposes, knowing You're planning something good.

A HOME BUILDER

A wise woman builds her home, but a foolish woman tears it down with her own hands.
PROVERBS 14:1 NLT

Worry has a domino effect. If you start fretting over something that has caught your attention and then voice your concern or act panic-stricken, chances are others around you will fall in with your anxiety. Everyone in your household, church, or workplace will come unglued.

Better to be a wise woman who builds up her home and her fellow travelers with a steady life of prayer and encouragement as well as an evident faith in God. When worries enter your thoughts, seek Jesus' face immediately. Ask Him to take on your troubles as you pick up His peace. Trust that He will see you through no matter what lies ahead or behind. Then you will be in a position to help others work through their own worries, mostly by being a calm, good listener, encouraging them when they need it, and giving wise advice when asked.

. . . .

Lord, help me be a wise woman, building up my home by giving You my worries and taking on Your peace.

RIGHT INTENTIONS

*Aim at and pursue righteousness (all that is
virtuous and good, right living, conformity to the
will of God in thought, word, and deed); [and
aim at and pursue] faith, love, [and] peace.*
2 TIMOTHY 2:22 AMPC

Setting your aims or intentions for the day (or your life) before your feet hit the floor may keep you from easily slipping into worry. So you *can* intend to not worry. But rather than going with a negative, why not set a positive intention that will leave no room for fretting. Consider what the apostle Paul tells Timothy to intend: "aim at and pursue" living God's way and go after "faith, love, [and] peace." No worries there!

Today, before you rise from your bed, make it your intention to live right, the way God would have you live. Make up your mind to pursue faith, love, and peace, and worry will lose its foothold.

The intentions you set are usually met.

. . . .

*Today, Lord, my intention is to pursue faith,
love, and peace with You by my side!*

YOUR GUIDE AND GUARDIAN

*"He found them in a. . .howling wasteland. He surrounded
them and watched over them; he guarded them
as he would guard his own eyes. Like an eagle that. . .
hovers over her young, so he spread his wings to take
them up and carried them safely on his pinions."*
DEUTERONOMY 32:10–11 NLT

Sometimes you may feel as if you're all alone in a desert, lost and unprotected, the wind howling all around you. You worry that you're too vulnerable, that there's no one able to help you.

Rest easy. God is with you. He's surrounding you, watching over you. He's guarding you as if you were the apple or pupil of His eye. He knows how fragile you can be and promises to protect you. Like a mother eagle, He's spreading His wings over you. He'll take you up and carry you, leading you to a better place where His promises will override your worries.

. . . .

*Thank You, Lord, for coming to meet me where
I am. Guard me as You do Your own eyes.
Carry me away to Your land of promise.*

YOUR BEST DEFENSE

*The Lord is my Rock, my Fortress, and my
Deliverer; my God, my keen and firm Strength
in Whom I will trust and take refuge, my Shield,
and the Horn of my salvation, my High Tower.*
PSALM 18:2 AMPC

If you're looking for a defense against worry, look no further than your Lord. That's what David did, and he became the apple of God's eye (see Psalm 17:8 ESV) even when and after he made some pretty major mistakes!

In Psalm 18, David begins by telling God how much he loves Him (see v. 1). Then he describes what God is to him—his Rock, Fortress, Deliverer, Strength, Shield, Horn (power), and High Tower. Then he sings, "I will call upon the Lord, Who is to be praised; so shall I be saved from my enemies" (Psalm 18:3 AMPC).

When worry gets out of hand, keeping you from doing what God would have you do, sing a song of praise to Him. Remind yourself of who He is, and He will save you!

. . . .

*My Rock and Deliverer, save me from my
worries as I sing a song of praise to You!*

BLESSED IN ASTONISHING WAYS

God can pour on the blessings in astonishing ways so that you're ready for anything and everything, more than just ready to do what needs to be done.
2 CORINTHIANS 9:8 MSG

George Müller ran an orphanage in England in the 1800s. One morning, there was no money, and the children's breakfast bowls and cups were empty. As the kids stood, waiting for their meal, Müller prayed, "Dear Father, we thank Thee for what Thou art going to give us to eat."

Then a baker, prompted by God, knocked on the door. His arms were filled with bread for the children. He was followed by a milkman whose cart had broken down in front of the orphanage. He wanted to give the kids cans of milk so he could empty and repair his wagon.

God knows and has what you need. Transform your worries about want into prayers for provisions, and you'll be blessed "in astonishing ways."

. . . .

Lord, bless me in astonishing ways
so that I may bless others in return.

KINGDOM-OF-HEAVEN BLESSING

Even if you suffer for doing what is right, God will reward you for it. So don't worry or be afraid of their threats. Instead, you must worship Christ as Lord of your life.
1 PETER 3:14–15 NLT

Today's verse, which says you're not to worry or be afraid when you're threatened, was written by the disciple Peter, who'd been both worried and afraid when Jesus was arrested. In fact, he went so far as to deny even knowing Jesus! But in the end, Peter was more devoted to Jesus than ever.

Jesus doesn't promise you a life without trouble, but He does promise you His peace and reward if you stick close to Him, doing what's right.

When you feel threatened by what others say and do as you live for Jesus, just keep Him and His words set in your mind and heart. Worship instead of worry, assured of your reward and God's kingdom-of-heaven blessing (see Matthew 5:10).

With You as my Lord and fortress, I need not worry or fear the words of others. Thank You, Lord, for blessing me as I follow You.

CHIN UP, WOMAN!

Energize the limp hands, strengthen the rubbery knees.
Tell fearful souls, "Courage! Take heart! GOD is here,
right here, on his way to put things right and redress
all wrongs. He's on his way! He'll save you!"
ISAIAH 35:3–4 MSG

It's good to have some Bible verses memorized, ones you can just call up during times of worry, stress, fear, or crises. Isaiah 35:3–4 are two of these verses. Find a Bible version of them that really speaks to your heart. Then use these verses when you start feeling anxious, when your hands are weak and your knees are about to give way.

Speak Isaiah's words into your soul to strengthen your body, mind, and spirit, rephrasing them if you need to. Say to yourself, "Chin up, woman. Be brave. Take heart. God is right here with you. He's going to put things right. He's on His way to save you!"

Remember, Jesus is your *Immanuel*, which means "God is with us" (see Matthew 1:23)! So don't panic—pray!

. . . .

Thank God You're with me, Jesus! With You
heading my way, I know You'll put things right!

NEVER SHAKEN

I will bless the LORD who guides me; even at night my heart instructs me. I know the LORD is always with me. I will not be shaken, for he is right beside me.
PSALM 16:7–8 NLT

These days, lots of businesses are open 24-7. But God has been open and available to His people day and night since they were created.

So if you have the all-powerful Creator constantly by your side, guiding you in the day and advising you in the night, whatever could you be worried about?

See things through God's eternal perspective. Your days are like a moment to Him. So live life to the fullest with no worries, fears, or anxieties to distract you or to keep you from the joy and peace that is yours in Christ.

God is with you. You will never be shaken. Let that stir your spirit into moving in rhythm with Him, filled with courage, peace, and joy, all the days of your life.

. . . .

I bless You, Lord, for guiding me, teaching me, and always being with me. I need not be shaken because You're beside me!

PARTNERING WITH GOD

*We are assured and know that [God being a partner in
their labor] all things work together and are [fitting into
a plan] for good to and for those who love God and
are called according to [His] design and purpose.*
ROMANS 8:28 AMPC

Romans 8:28 says that everything that happens in your life—
whether good or bad, within or out of your control—happens
for a reason and according to God's plan and that He will make
everything work out for your good.

That can be hard to accept sometimes, yet that doesn't mean
it isn't true. After all, it was true for Joseph, who'd been put in a
pit by loved ones, sold as a slave, sent to the dungeon, and yet
ended up the number two man in Egypt!

Instead of worrying about what may or may not happen, rest in
the assurance that no matter what happens, God will work it out
for good. Remember, God can do anything. Your job? Trust Him.

. . . .

*Lord, with You as my partner, I know all things will
work out for good. On that I stake my faith!*

IN GOD'S HANDS

God is our refuge and strength, always ready to help in times of trouble. So we will not fear when earthquakes come and the mountains crumble into the sea. Let the oceans roar and foam. Let the mountains tremble as the waters surge!
PSALM 46:1–3 NLT

Sometimes it may feel as if your world is falling apart—literally! The weather has turned wacky; mountainous glaciers are melting, volcanoes erupting, cities flooding, forests burning. . . . It's enough to make any normal woman worry.

Yet, because you're a daughter of the Most High God, you don't have to be anxious or fear anything because you can go to God for refuge. In Him you will find all the strength and help you need to get through anything and everything.

So rest easy. Pray to God. Tell Him you know He's in control and somehow everything will be all right. You don't need to know the details. Leave them—and everything else that's on your mind—in His hands.

. . . .

*Thank You, Lord, for always being there, ready
to shield, strengthen, and help me. Because
of You I have peace and courage!*

PULLED BY PROMISES

With promises like this to pull us on, dear friends, let's make a clean break with everything that defiles or distracts us, both within and without. Let's make our entire lives fit and holy temples for the worship of God.
2 CORINTHIANS 7:1 MSG

God has a plan for your life. He wants you to live for Him, to trust Him, to base your words and actions on His promises, to expect good to come out of all things.

God wants you, His darling daughter, to be strong and fit. For that, you need "a calm and undisturbed mind and heart," which are "the life and health of the body" (Proverbs 14:30 AMPC).

For God's pleasure and your own health and welfare, make a clean break from the worries that distract you. Go to God, trusting Him with your concerns. Dig into His promises, believing them and making them your own. Live in God's reality, and you'll be living the life He dreamed for you.

· ·

Help me be a fit temple for You, Lord. Give me the calm mind I yearn for in You.

SCRIPTURE INDEX

OLD TESTAMENT